Eastern Front Sniper

GREENHILL SNIPER LIBRARY

Available:

Snipers At War: An Equipment and Operations History

John Walter

Forthcoming:

The Sniper Encyclopaedia: An Illustrated History of World Sniping

John Walter

Russian Sniper

Evgeni Nikolaev

Lady Death: The Memoirs of Stalin's Sniper

Lyudmila Pavlichenko

Eastern Front Sniper

The Life of Matthäus Hetzenauer

Roland Kaltenegger

Foreword by
Martin Pegler

Translated by
Geoffrey Brooks

Greenhill Books

Eastern Front Sniper
This edition published in 2017 by
Greenhill Books,
c/o Pen & Sword Books Ltd,
47 Church Street, Barnsley,
S. Yorkshire, S70 2AS

www.greenhillbooks.com
contact@greenhillbooks.com

ISBN: 978–1–78438–216–2

First published in German as
Gefreiter der Reserve Matthäus Hetzenauer:
Vom erfolgreichsten Scharfschützen der Wehrmacht
zum Ritterkreuzträger

Flechsig Verlag, Beethovenstraße 5 B,
D-97080 Würzburg, Germany
www.verlagshaus.com

CIP data records for this title are available from the British Library

Printed and bound in Malta by Gutenberg Press

Typeset in 9.5/14.5 pt ITC Bookman Light

Contents

Contents

Foreword

Matthäus Hetzenauer, Scharfschutzen

WHEN I WAS INTERVIEWING a high-scoring Second World War British sniper some years ago, I asked what sort of men made the best snipers. He told me that they were not the 'life-and-soul of the party' type and in the unlikely event one was there at all, he would be the quiet one sitting in the corner, probably drinking fruit juice and observing everyone else. Extrovert snipers were a liability to themselves and their comrades and seldom had a long service life. Snipers can generally be typified as reflective, observant men, who deliberated carefully about things before acting. It was how they survived. Sniping is the most physically and mentally demanding of any military role and in World War Two sniper casualty rates were around 80 per cent. The fact that Matthäus Hetzenauer became the highest-scoring Axis sniper and lived to tell the tale says a great deal about the sort of man he was. Much of the detail of his life after the war remains unknown, although his family tell of a quiet man who loved the Alpine region in which he had been brought up, but did not talk about his experiences. However, there must have been iron under his skin for not only did he survive the bitter Eastern Front campaign, but remarkably also the privations of five years of captivity and forced labour. Some idea of the harshness of life in the Soviet prison camps can be seen from current estimates that of the near three million Germans captured by the end of the war, almost one million died in captivity.

As is so often the case with snipers, personal details about their lives are sparse; very few wrote autobiographies and those who did often fictionalised their accounts, in part to protect others, but also to play down their own role. The fact is that probably 99 per cent of snipers have not left any written testimony as to their involvement in the fighting. Even long after the war, the majority were extremely reluctant to talk about what they did. Those Allied snipers whom I have interviewed spoke to me only under a mutual understanding of the strictest confidence and much of what I have been told has never been published out of respect for their wishes. Matthäus Hetzenauer was no exception. Although his compatriot and fellow Austrian sniper Josef Allerberger did collaborate with Dr Albrecht Wacker to write a fictionalised account of his life in 2000 (*Im Auge des Jägers*) this was a very rare event, but Allerberger's war service is interesting in that it parallels that of Hetzenauer to an extraordinary degree for they served in the same division and on the same battle fronts and they knew each other well. Thus they would both have seen and experienced much the same events. It is believed that Hetzenauer only ever gave one interview on the subject of his shooting, in the magazine *Truppendienst* ('Troop Service') in 1967, and I have based much of the information below on his comments.

The Rifles

A technical explanation of the sniping war on the Eastern Front might be of interest to the reader, as it saw the greatest amount and the most deadly sniping of any theatre of the whole war. Both sides began the fighting with the minimum of sniping equipment, although the Soviet Army was initially the better equipped and trained of the two. This was in part due to the appalling losses inflicted on it during the brief Winter War against the Finns between November 1939 and March 1940. The Finnish Army fielded a large number of snipers and expert riflemen, against whom the Soviets had little or no defence. It was somewhat ironic that the rifles the Finns used were actually Soviet-designed Mosin Nagants, albeit a re-worked variant called the M.27, mostly assembled in Finland with high-quality barrels supplied by Swiss and German companies. Some were equipped with telescopic sights, but many

An early-war photo of a German sniper making use of a captured Mosin Nagant/PU scope combination.

were not. In the hands of the expert hunters who had transferred their skills to the Finnish Army, this mattered not a bit. Indeed, many snipers regarded the telescopic sights as a hindrance in the bitterly cold conditions. This was due to several factors: a scope needed to be kept warm, often in a pouch worn next to the sniper's body, but when fitted to a rifle and used, sudden exposure to the cold would result in it instantly fogging up, rendering it useless. The adjustment drums could freeze solid, as could the reticules (crosshairs), and the mounting screws become brittle in the cold. The highest scoring of all the Finnish snipers, Simo Häyhä, or as the Russians called him *Belaya Smert* ('White Death'), achieved the majority of his 505 official kills with an un-scoped rifle.

The Russians were not devoid of snipers or sniping rifles during the Winter War, however; they did have small numbers of trained men equipped with a scoped version of the venerable Mosin Nagant M1891/30 rifle, but there were insufficient of both to deal with the Finns and the snipers themselves were poorly

A Mosin Nagant rifle with the early pattern PE scope. NRA

trained. The rifles were fitted with a 4-power scope known as the PE (with a later improved model called the PEM), which had been copied from a World War One German pattern made by Emil Busch AG, and these had been in production since 1931. It was physically a comparatively large instrument but it did have excellent optics.

However, it was clear after the war that there were huge gaps in the preparation and employment of Russian snipers. As a result they set up a massive training programme and embarked on the production of very large quantities of scoped rifles. Germany meanwhile had been held back by the post-World War One restrictions imposed upon it by the Versailles Treaty, which severely limited the development and production of military weapons, naturally including sniping rifles. The Germans managed to evade this to some extent by retaining numbers of Great War-era Gewehr 98 (Gew.98) sniping rifles. Experience during the war had shown that these original long-barrelled rifles were too cumbersome in combat and the extra barrel length achieved little in the way of improved accuracy. As a result, most of them were modified post-war by being shortened to carbine (K98a) configuration by having six inches (150mm) lopped off the barrel, bringing it down to a more manageable 23 inches (590 mm).

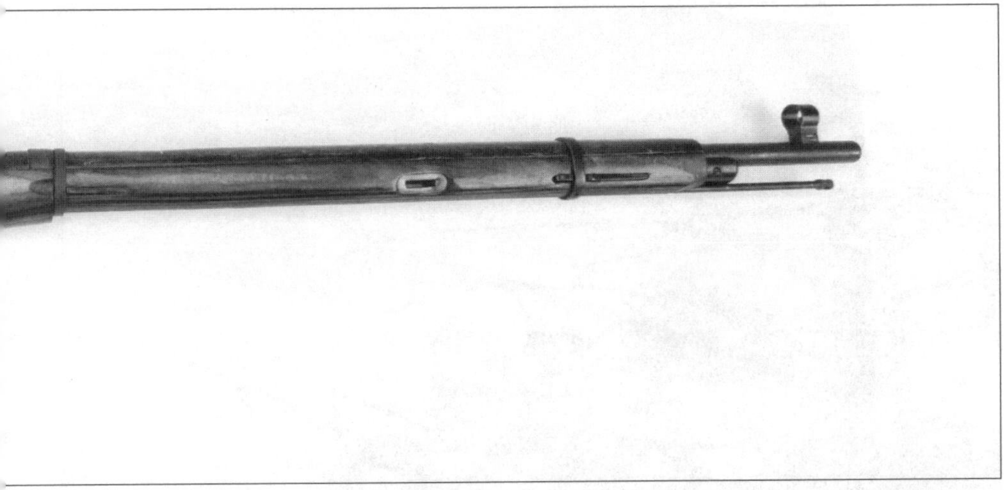

Within the German military, only the SS had made any attempt to continue with a sniper training programme through the 1930s and they developed the first in a long line of sniping rifles, which were based on the new carbine Mauser adopted in 1934, the Karabiner 98k (K98k). This was, to all effects, a re-worked K98a but with a fractionally longer barrel of 23.6 inches (600 mm). They also used whatever stock they could find of older Gew.98s and they adapted them for sniping by means of fitting a side-rail mounted scope, but available numbers were small. In fact, early photographs from the invasion of Russia show German soldiers with some original long-barrelled Gew.98 rifles that had clearly been brought out of retirement to provide some form of sniper armament. By the time that Hetzenauer reached the front line in late 1944 the situation had changed considerably although Germany still lagged behind in some respects.

By 1944 the Germans were manufacturing a bewildering range of sniping rifles, with some seven different major variants of scopes and mounts fitted to the Mauser K98k and two semi-automatic rifles, the Gewehr 41 and Selbstladegewehr 43 (Gew.41/43). This does not take into account specialist rifles, such as the Sturmgewehr (Stg) family of early assault rifles. Neither was the situation helped by Adolf Hitler's insistence that from 1941 a small 1.5-power optical sight, the Zielfernrohr 41 (Zf.41) be manufactured in large numbers for general issue to

German soldiers at the start of the invasion of Russia, 1941. The sniper, right, holds a shortened Mauser K98a fitted with Great War-era scope.

troops, to provide the men with some sharpshooting ability. It was generally disliked by the snipers themselves and was not used at the German sniping schools as part of their instructional process, but the production of over 100,000 during the war seriously diluted the ability of the optical manufacturers to concentrate on increasing the production of better models.

In terms of what was the best of the German scope/mount combinations, without doubt the bolt-action K98k Mauser rifle equipped with the high or low Turret Mount was the most highly regarded in terms of strength, reliability and practicality. Indeed, the mounting system was generally believed to be unbreakable, no mean feat where soldiers are concerned.

Unlike Allerberger, who initially used a captured Soviet Mosin Nagant sniping rifle, Hetzenauer was issued from the start with a K98k Mauser rifle. He said that his favoured combination was

'A K98k with 6-power sight' and the image of him reproduced on the cover of this book, smiling self-consciously at the camera, clearly shows this rifle and scope combination. Although the Mausers predominantly used a 4-power Zeiss scope some 6-power models were available but, oddly, it was these scopes that proved to be their primary weakness. They were a World War One-era design which had only a single elevation drum. Windage adjustment, to allow for sidewinds, had to be done by means of a fiddly worm screw on the rear mount. It was slow, awkward and impossible to do under combat situations. Nevertheless, once set up, the scope was durable, accurate and, if removed, could be replaced without materially affecting the zeroing of the rifle.

In 1939 Russia had abandoned the old PE/PEM designs in favour of a simpler and smaller 3.5-power PU scope. It too had excellent optics and large, simple range and elevation drums which were a boon in the cold, when gloves were a prerequisite. Soviet arms factories were turning out rifles and telescopes at

A converted Mauser Gew.98 with an early short side-rail mount and 4-power Zeiss scope.

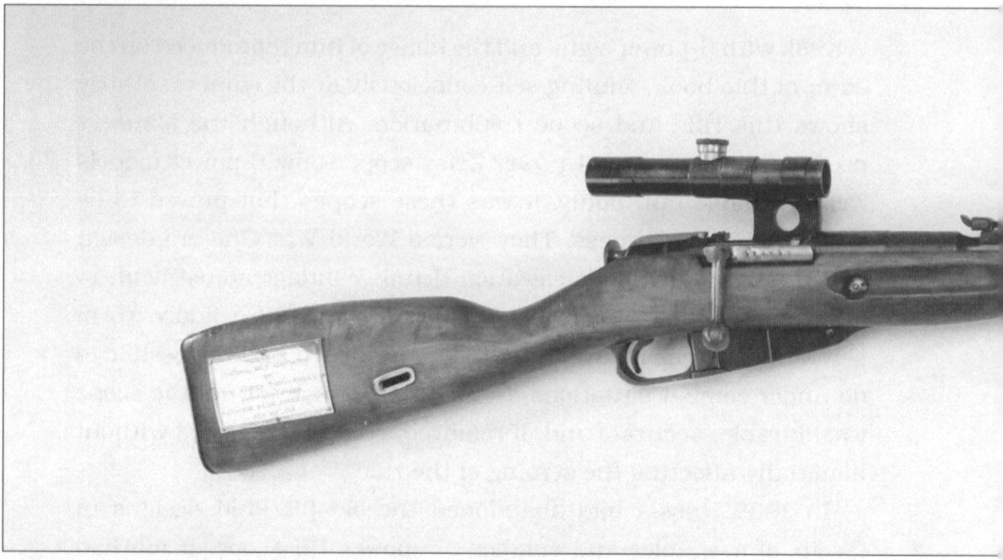

A Mosin Nagant rifle with the later PU scope. The large thumbscrew for mounting, and the crude mount itself, are typical of wartime Soviet mass-production.

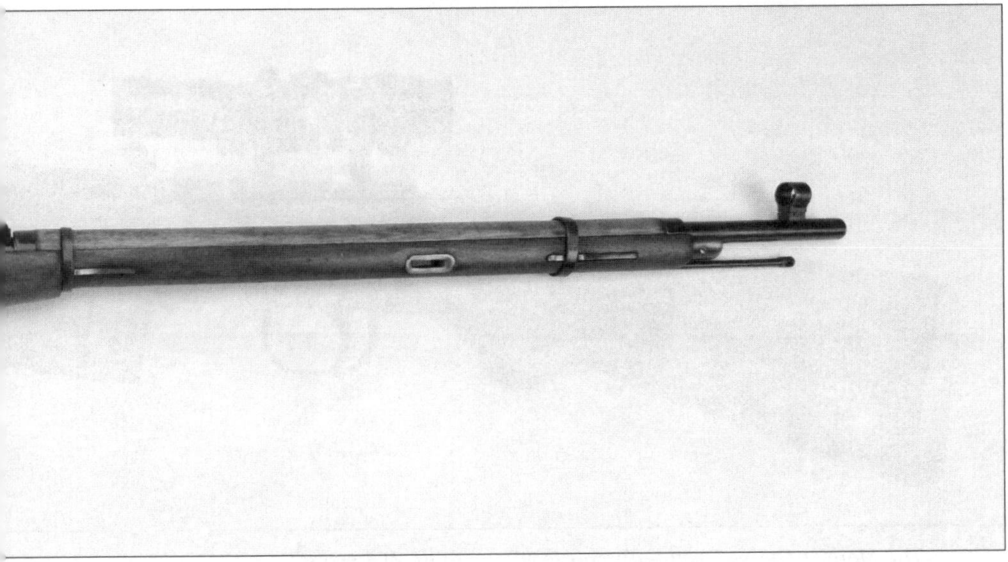

A captured Mosin Nagant rifle with PU scope. NRA

an incredible rate (between 1941 and 1943 in excess of 300,000 Mosins equipped with PU scopes). The Russian PU combination did also suffer from flaws, though; whereas the scope was a brilliant design, the mounting system for it relied upon a screwed block that held the scope and its mount against a backplate fitted to the receiver of the rifle. It was difficult to remove easily – the big thumbscrew was vulnerable to damage and could shear in extreme cold. From personal experience, the author can also confirm that once it was removed, it was seldom possible to replace it without re-zeroing the rifle.

The semi-automatics

In 1938, the Russians had fielded a semi-automatic rifle, the Samozaryadnaya Vintovka Tokareva (Tokarev Self-loading Rifle) or SVT-38, of which a small number were modified for sniping use by means of a fitting a neat, U-shaped mounting bracket to the rear of the receiver to hold a PU scope. It was soon replaced with an improved version, the SVT-40, which used the same optical system. These were manufactured in significant numbers with

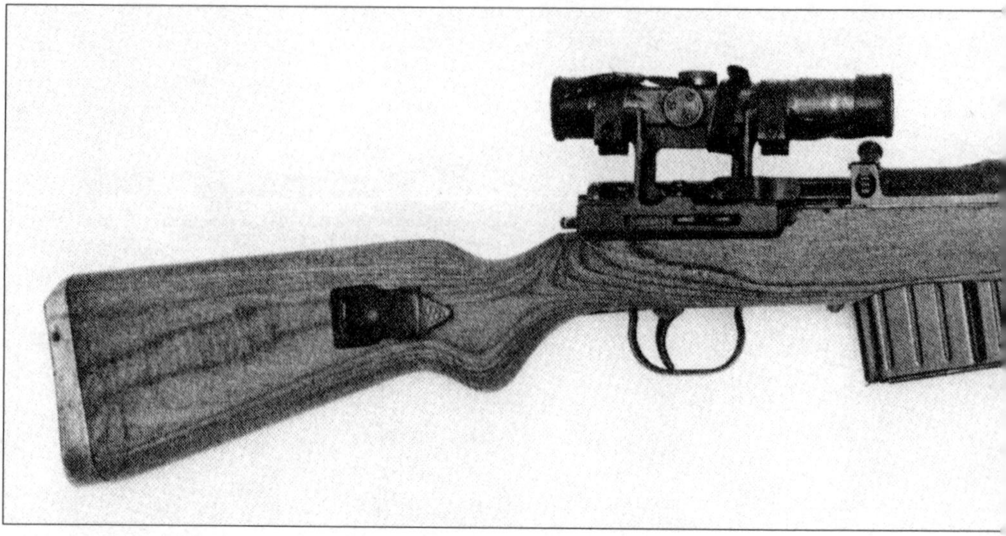

The Mauser Gew.43 semi-automatic rifle with its Zf.4 scope.

around 52,000 sniper variants produced until production ceased in 1942.

Although the SVT-40 developed a reputation for unreliability, this was more often due to poor maintenance than sub-standard manufacture and when used by snipers, who were generally very disciplined in the care of their rifles, they generally performed well. The Germans took a great deal of interest in these rifles and initially produced the Mauser-designed Gewehr 41, which was heavy, complicated and unreliable. Undeterred, they produced a new model, the Selbstladegewehr Model 43 (Gew.43), which was an improvement, but arguably not by much. However, it was equipped with the first of a new generation of optical sights, the excellent 4-power Zielfernrohr 4 (Zf.4) scope. This owed much to the compact Soviet PU design, incorporating easily operated range and elevation drums, but unlike the Russian rifle, whose scope mounting was crude, the Zf.4 used a practical quick-release thumb-operated locking mechanism on a sliding side mount that owed much to the early side-rail system; Hetzenauer did use a Gew.43 under some circumstances.

The problem with semi-automatic rifles, of whatever type, was that they were never capable of achieving the same level

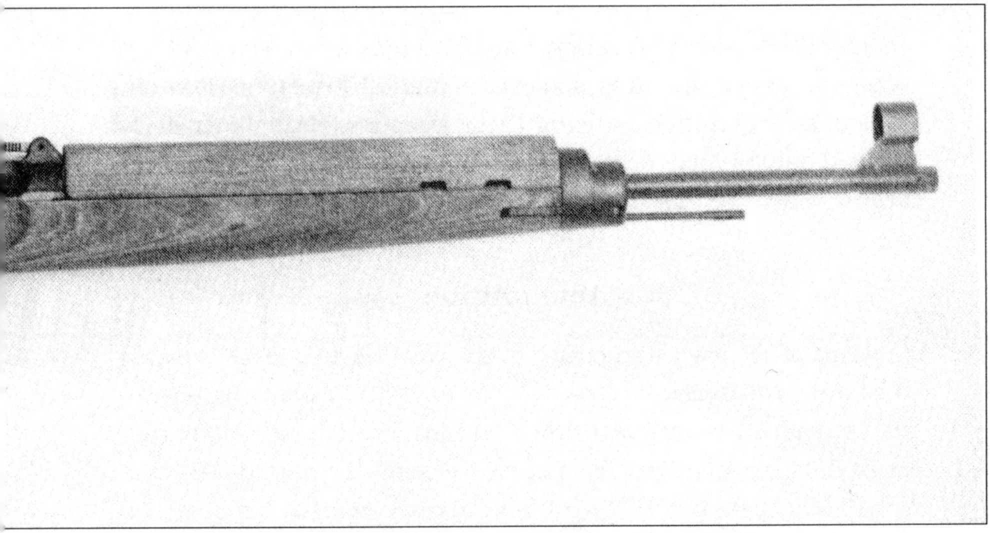

of accuracy as a bolt-action rifle. Whilst a Mauser rifle was an excellent sniping weapon out to 700 or 800 metres (770–875 yards) in the hands of a good sniper, the semi-automatics were effective to 400 or perhaps 500 metres (440–550 yards). This was due mainly to the large number of moving parts and the difficulty that the factories had in ensuring that every part was manufactured to near-perfect dimensions, a virtually impossible task when mass-production techniques were used. At least a bolt-action rifle, with its minimum moving parts, could be re-worked by a skilled gunsmith or armourer to create a smoothly operating and consistently accurate weapon, which was an exceedingly difficult and lengthy task to undertake with a semi-automatic. However, there were times when their use had its advantages. In house-to-house or street fighting, the high rate of fire made up for the lack of range and this was proven time and again in pitched battles or in cities such as Stalingrad.

For the German snipers, the Gew.43 often proved invaluable during mass attacks by Soviet infantry. Indeed, at close ranges many snipers on both sides resorted to the use of sub-machine guns. Allerberger used his Gew.43 to grim but deadly effect by deliberately shooting attacking Russians in the stomach, their screams invariably causing comrades to falter and fall back. This required a high rate of fire that was difficult to achieve with the comparatively slow bolt-action, as the attacks were often made en masse at very close ranges, sometimes under 100 metres. However, although he admitted to using these weapons, Hetzenauer dryly pointed out, 'Snipers do not need a semi-automatic weapon if they are correctly used as snipers.'

Ammunition

In terms of accuracy and power, there was little to choose between the Soviet and German rifles. The Mosin and SVT both chambered the original 1891-designed 7.62 x 54 mm tapered, rimmed bottle-necked cartridge that reached a velocity of around 797 m/sec (2,600 fps). The 7.92 x 57 mm Mauser rimless bottlenecked cartridge which dated from 1905 achieved 820 m/sec (2,700 fps). Both used a streamlined boat-tailed (tapered) pointed nosed bullet, the Mauser having a heavy 12.8 g (197 grain) bullet, as opposed to the Mosin's 11.7 g (181 grain), although both produced nearly identical muzzle energy. In practical terms, this gave the rifles a *theoretical* ability to kill at ranges in excess of 2,000 metres, (2,200 yards). However, combat sniping is not about theories, but what is achievable – shooting distances were considerably under the maximum range as will be seen from Hetzenauer's later comments.

Much has been written about the use of 'special purpose' ammunition by snipers on the Eastern Front, such as tracer, armour-piercing and explosive bullets. Ammunition quality, in terms of consistent performance, was vital and every sniper would zero his rifle to a particular batch of cartridges, which he would then use exclusively, confident that each successive shot would have the same point of impact. The problem with using anything other than standard heavy-bullet ball ammunition ('schweres Spitzgeschoss' or s.S) was that the point of impact could be quite significantly different, so tracer or armour-piercing rounds would require the rifle to be re-zeroed for use at anything other than very close ranges. In the front line the shooter could not easily or quickly adjust his scope to compensate for this. Therefore the use of these types of ammunition was generally reserved only for very specific tasks.

When asked about his use of different forms of ammunition, Hetzenauer was quite informative, believing that tracer (Spitzgeschoss mit Stahlkern und Leuchtspur or 'Sm.K.L') was dangerous to use, as it could reveal the location of the sniper. 'Tracer ammunition was mainly used for practice shooting as well as ranging at various distances. For this reason every sniper carried a few tracer cartridges with him.' He noted that because of the variable accuracy of such ammunition he had to rely on, '. . . my own judgement and experience; when necessary, I used tracer ammunition to determine wind drift. I was well prepared for sidewinds by my training at Seetaleralp where we often practised in strong winds.' As to armour-piercing (Spitzgeschoss mit Stahlkern or S.m.K), this did have its uses as Soviet machine gunners and observers often used steel loophole plates. His experience was that S.m.K ammunition was useful as he often fought against machine gunners with protective shields on their weapons.

Interestingly he also used unspecified variants of the German Panzerbüchse anti-tank rifles (probably Panzerbüchse Models 35, 38 or 39), which were already obsolete for use against tank armour, but their high-velocity armour-piercing ammunition made them ideal for softer targets such as bunkers or loopholes. However, he added, 'I could hit small targets only up to 300 metres [330 yards] since dispersion was considerably larger than with the K98. Besides, it was very heavy and clumsy and was not suitable as a sniper weapon. I did not use it against unarmoured targets.' As these rifles were fitted with ordinary iron sights and weighed anything up to 11.5 kg (25.5 lb) accurate shooting at 300 metres was no mean feat.

With regards to the controversial use of explosive ammunition (B-Patrone), which had been outlawed under international law for use against human targets, he was unequivocal. These rounds were used but only for observation. The bullet strike emitted a cloud of blue-white smoke that was observable at a range of up to 2,000 yards (1,830 metres) but it would also burn for some seconds and this proved unexpectedly useful against Russian thatched farmhouses. 'Upon impact a small puff of smoke could be seen which allowed good observation. By this means, we could force the enemy to leave wooden houses by setting fire to them.'

Training

There were at least three sniper training schools in Germany and one for the Austrian Mountain Division in Seetaleralp, the Institute of Military Training, which still exists and where Hetzenauer trained. As in the Allied armies, the rifle that a sniper was given in training was for his personal use and snipers disliked anyone else touching or firing their weapon. Every man set up his rifle to suit his own particular physical requirements and no two rifles were identical due to every individual having his own eyesight requirements, grip preference and shooting style.

German doctrine for sniper training differed slightly from that of the British, for example, as weapon training and fieldcraft were merged into one, and not taught as compartmentalised units. Training in the Alps also provided a big advantage for the weather conditions often mirrored those of the Eastern Front, with intense cold, snow, strong winds and the difficult requirements of shooting at high altitudes, where distances were hard to estimate and ballistic performance altered by the thin air. Across the wide valleys, where the snow blotted out features, estimating range was fraught with difficulties. If a human being could be seen, then a distance relating to his height could be calculated using a chart or gradations on binoculars, but miscalculating by a matter of a few metres would result in a complete miss. This was one reason why snipers tended to leave their scopes set at a combat range of around 300 metres (330 yards) and use the mouth of the target as an aiming point. Should the range be over or under-estimated, the bullet would strike either the forehead or chest, both of which would result in death. Where windage was concerned, they simply used their judgement by 'aiming off' to one side or the other to allow the wind to carry the bullet into the target; this required some considerable skill. In addition, the higher the altitude, the flatter the trajectory of the bullet and the greater adjustment required than at sea level on the telescopic sight, but even for the

A posed photo of a remarkably clean sniper with a newly issued K98k and high Turret Mount scope. The tiny windage adjusting screw is just visible at the bottom of the rear mount, just above the bolt.

best snipers, shooting at high altitude or in a strong wind was generally nothing more than a waste of ammunition.

On the subject of who made the best snipers, Hetzenauer was in agreement with the evaluation done in World War One. 'Only people born for individual fighting, such as hunters, forest rangers, even poachers, etc.' He added that: 'Besides the generally known qualities of a sniper it is especially important to be able to outwit the enemy. The better "tactician of detail" wins in combat against enemy snipers.' In other words, snipers needed to be intelligent enough to work out their own strategy and be obsessive in their attention to details such as camouflage, positioning, movement and so on. 'The exemption from other duties (such as fatigues, sentry duty etc.) contributed vitally to the achievement of high scores.' However, unlike Britain, where only volunteers were accepted as snipers, a good shot in the German Army could quite literally be plucked from the front line and returned to Germany for training, as indeed happened to Hetzenauer.

Aside from shooting training and fieldcraft, the art of camouflage was one of the most highly regarded disciplines and the Germans were taught to make maximum use of any local plants or other material that would provide them with adequate cover. In winter, white smocks, rifles wrapped in bandages and white-daubed faces were commonplace and Sepp Allerberger was famous for using an umbrella painted to match whatever the local terrain happened to be.

There was also considerable use made of deception and ruses on both sides. Hetzenauer used dummies, sometimes equipped with rifles that could be remotely fired using a lanyard, as well as the old trick of slowly raising a helmet on a stick, although this tended to catch out only the less experienced enemy snipers. He made the point that he never used a steel loophole plate as they were fixed in position and too vulnerable to enemy observation. To watch the enemy, his favoured optical item was a pair of German 6 x 30 binoculars but when in the lines close to the enemy or in no-man's land he predominately used a captured Soviet periscope.

Accuracy

An old axiom for shooters has always been 'If you can't see it, you can't hit it.' This has never been more true than where sniping is concerned and the better the optics, the higher the chance of making a hit. One of the problems besetting both sides was the use of scopes with thick vertical and horizontal reticules. This meant that at longer ranges, a human body was effectively obscured by the vertical post, providing the sniper with only a very small target area. Hetzenauer stated that the 4-power scopes were sufficient up to 400 metres, the 6-power to 1,000 and that he would guarantee a head shot at 400 only with the more powerful scope. He believed that he would also be able to hit a standing man at 600 metres, but he admitted that only the best snipers could achieve this on a regular basis.

His comments regarding the general efficiency of German snipers are interesting for he believed that, 'The majority of snipers could hit with absolute certainty *only* within a range of

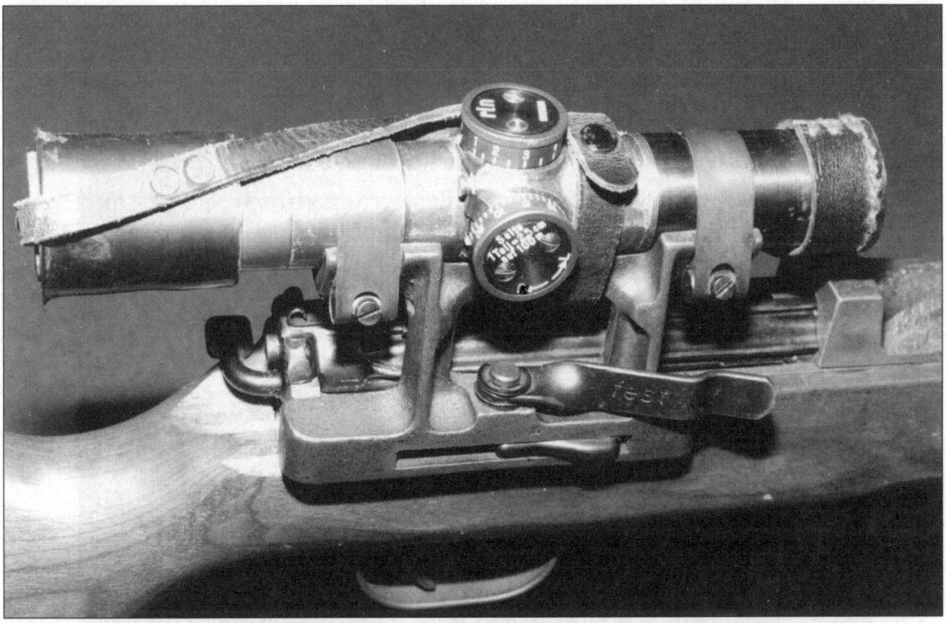

A close-up of the Zf.4 showing its compact size.

400 metres due to their limited skills; however, in most cases they waited until the enemy was closer or [they] approached the enemy in order to better choose the target.' He added that the majority of his own hits, 65 per cent, were also at under 400 metres, 'since targets could be better evaluated with respect to merit at that distance. At longer ranges hitting was still possible but I could not distinguish if the target was worthwhile.' He has often been misquoted about the range of his longest shot, but in the interview he pointed out that the 1,000-metre range at which he fired at a Russian soldier on one occasion meant he did not actually hit him, as 'Positive hits were not possible, but [firing was] necessary under certain circumstances in order to show the enemy that he was not safe even at that distance.' In common with most snipers, his preference was always the bolt-action rifle and he confirmed that he 'almost never' needed or wanted to fire a quick second shot, one of the few advantages that a semi-automatic possessed over a bolt-action weapon. Because of the confidence he had in his accuracy, he felt that a single shot from one location was sufficient, as any further shots could well betray his position.

A photo taken through the lens of a Zeiss scope, showing the thick reticules, with the wide centre-post.

Combat tactics

Despite the experience gained by officers in the First World War, who by 1918 looked like ordinary soldiers, in World War Two Soviet officers still often dressed so that they were easily recognisable by their men and this made them easy prey for snipers. Soviet snipers often commented that they shot the men who had thin legs, as they were invariably officers! Primary targets were of course unit commanders and on many occasions Hetzenauer worked his way through the enemy's lines prior to an attack specifically to target the officers and observers of artillery units, because 'I had to shoot at the enemy's commanders and gunners because our own forces would have been too weak in number and ammunition without this support.' He also aided his men during assaults by shooting machine gunners and anti-tank crews and he realised that selecting his targets carefully was a vital part of his effective employment. He said that,

The greatest success for snipers did not lie in the number of hits but in the damage caused to the enemy by shooting commanders or other important men. As to the merit of individual hits, the sniper's best results could always be obtained in defence, since the target could be better recognised with respect to its importance by careful observation. Regarding target numbers, the best results could usually be obtained in defence since the enemy attacked several times during the day . . .

Great successes during enemy attacks [were achieved] since commanders could often be recognised and shot at long range due to their special clothing and gear, such as belts crossed on the chest, white camouflage in winter and so on.

A Mountain Division sniper with a K98k and high Turret Mount scope.

Hetzenauer also pointed out that his orders varied depending on the type of combat he faced. A large attack provided him with any number of possible targets, a smaller one or an assault by his own company was often accompanied by strict orders to shoot only at 'worthwhile targets'. He went on to say that,

> As a rule, the sniper watched for significant targets from the break of day and remained in position until dusk with few breaks. We were often in position in front of our own lines in order to fight the enemy. We were forced to remain without provisions or replacements in such advanced positions. During alarms or enemy attacks, a good sniper did not shoot at just any target but only the most important ones such as commanders, gunners etc.

His understanding of the psychological importance of such specific shooting was well illustrated when on one notable occasion he repeatedly shot the commanders of an attacking Soviet company, killing eight in one day!

His comment about shooting at dawn and dusk is important, as these times were generally known as 'snipers' light' because the magnifying light-gathering ability of the telescopic sights was sufficient to enable kills to be made when the unaided human eye could not discern a target and when enemy soldiers were more careless about exposing themselves. During the retreat through Russia and operating as rearguards, sniper teams of six to eight men often worked in conjunction with machine guns to cover the sound of their rifles and this could delay an enemy advance for several hours, whilst the Russians brought up heavy weapons to dislodge them. This usually provided the rearguard with time to slip away. If they did not manage to escape, they could expect no quarter to be given.

Of course, enemy infantry were not the most problematical of the Soviet troops for German snipers to deal with, for the Soviets fielded some excellent snipers who were themselves the scourge of the German lines. Counter-sniping was thus a major occupation of the *Scharfschutzen* and Hetzenauer had this to say about the task: 'As soon as enemy snipers appeared we fought them until

A picture that illustrates the difficulties of shooting in high, snow-covered terrain.

they were eliminated; we also suffered great losses.' What lay behind this terse comment can only be imagined as many sniper duels were fought over several days, while each man attempted to outwit the other. Sometimes the tiniest of errors, such as a lens catching the sunlight, or an involuntary movement of the head or hand would result in a bullet to the head.

As to the official observation of his kills, as with all snipers this was something of a grey area, for to be credited with a kill any shot that a German sniper made had to be observed by an officer, an NCO or two other soldiers. As much of his sniping was done covertly from hides with just himself and perhaps one observer, there was no means of accurately quantifying the number of hits made by

Hetzenauer or any other sniper for that matter. Officially, his tally was 345. Unofficially, his actual number could well be double this. Had the Russians been aware of who they had captured in 1945, there is no doubt that he would have been summarily executed. The fact that snipers never wore any identifying insignia on their uniforms, nor carried documents detailing their training may well have saved his life; otherwise there is little doubt that he would not have lived to return to his beloved Tyrol.

Martin Pegler

All illustrations in the above Preface are from the Martin Pegler Collection, aside from those marked NRA, which are reproduced by courtesy of the National Rifle Association Museum Collection, Fairfax, Virginia.

Prologue

'AFTER A SNIPER'S COURSE, Hetzenauer came to 7th Company, 144th Mountain Rifle Regiment, which, as part of 3rd Mountain Division, had earlier been involved in the most bitter fighting for the Nikopol bridgehead west of the River Dnieper. With this company Hetzenauer experienced the hard-fought retreats between Ingulez and Bug in Romania, in eastern Hungary and in Slovakia. The war ended for this sorely tried division in the Schwarzwasser/Teschen area of Czechoslovakia. During all these battles Hetzenauer, meanwhile promoted to *Gefreiter*, was continually used as a sniper in his company's defensive sections and was compelled almost daily to engage in duels with Russian snipers and machine-gun crews. He often lay in wait for hours with his rifle ready to fire, despite cold and damp, knowing that any careless movement could mean a wound or death for himself. The sniper on this side or that was the lone warrior with the best nerves and the sharpest eye. Gefreiter Matthäus Hetzenauer thus became the most successful sniper of the entire German Wehrmacht. He emerged 346 times as victor and amongst the approximately 7,200 Knight's Cross holders. He was the only Wehrmacht soldier to have received this decoration as a sniper.[1] He is also the only soldier of the former Wehrmacht proved by an official document to have been awarded the Sniper's Badge in Gold.'

This extract is taken from the book of honour of the military 'Holy Land' of Tyrol entitled *High Awards for Bravery to Tyroleans in*

1. Karl Ruef later amended his comment that Hetzenauer was the only sniper to have received the Knight's Cross. For the award of the Knight's Cross to snipers Obergefreiter Josef Allerberger and Oberjäger Jakob Hechl, see Chapter 6, below. Regarding the supposed final rank of *Gefreiter* for Hetzenauer, see Translator's Introduction below.

VERÖFFENTLICHUNGEN DES INNSBRUCKER STADTARCHIVS

Schriftleitung: Franz-Heinz Hye

Neue Folge, Band 6

HOHE TAPFERKEITSAUSZEICHNUNGEN AN TIROLER IM ZWEITEN WELTKRIEG

von

Wilhelm Eppacher und Karl Ruef

Innsbruck 1975

Herausgeber und Verleger: Stadtmagistrat Innsbruck

Title page of High Awards for Bravery to Tyroleans in the Second World War *by Wilhelm Eppacher and Karl Ruef*, .

the Second World War composed by no less a person than the Tyrolean Knight's Cross holder and later publisher Oberst Karl Ruef.[1] Amongst his most significant works are the wartime diaries of the 3rd Mountain Division of General Eduard Dietl, sometimes known to military history as 'The Hero of Narvik',[2] and those of the 6th Mountain Division of General Ferdinand Schörner, who became eventually the only *Generalfeldmarschall* of the German mountain troops.[3]

1. Eppacher, Wilhelm, & Ruef, Karl, *Hohe Tapferkeitsauszeichnungen an Tiroler im Zweiten Weltkrieg*, Innsbruck, 1975, as amended.
2. Kaltenegger, Roland, *Generaloberst Eduard Dietl*, Würzburg, 2012.
3. Kaltenegger, Roland, *Generalfeldmarschall Ferdinand Schörner*, Würzburg, 2014.

Translator's Introduction

'Gefreiter Matthäus Hetzenauer became the most successful sniper of the entire German Wehrmacht. He emerged 346 times as victor . . .'

This paragraph, taken from the Prologue above, requires clarification. Matthäus Hetzenauer was the indeed most successful Wehrmacht sniper with 346 confirmed hits – *as from the date of the institution of the Sniper Badge on 1 September 1944.* Any previous credits for all snipers were 'sacrificed to the *Führer*' in exchange for the Iron Cross Second Class. Obergefreiter Josef Allerberger, also of 144th Mountain Rifle Regiment, served as a sniper from early August 1943 and all his confirmed kills during the next thirteen months were 'sacrificed to the *Führer*' in this way. *As from the institution of the Sniper Badge on 1 September 1944*, Allerberger had 257 confirmed kills, but as he said, 'the actual number was inestimably greater' (Wacker, Albrecht, *Sniper on the Eastern Front*, p. 143).

Hetzenzauer's Rank

The final page of the plates in this volume shows the display of Matthäus Hetzenauer's badges, orders and decorations, and his photograph wearing them is on the first plates page. Author Kaltenegger states in this book that Hetzenauer was promoted to the rank of *Gefreiter* on 11 April 1945, and Karl Ruef has his final rank as *Gefreiter.* This cannot be correct. After passing out from Sniper School, Hetzenauer's rank as a trained specialist upon joining 3rd Mountain Division in July 1944 would have been *Gefreiter* (trained private soldier). Hetzenauer even told the *Tiroler Volksblatt* that he was a *Gefreiter*. Under the subheading '*Ein Scharfschütze*' the Kufstein edition of the paper of 23 February 1945 reproduced on page 113 below has a report beginning, 'Several snipers, amongst them *Gefreiter* Hetzenauer . . .' and twenty-three lines lower down he calls himself '*Gefreiter* Hetzenauer'.

Since Hetzenauer's rank was definitely *Gefreiter* on 10 March 1945 as stated on several occasions in the official document recommending him for the award of the Knight's Cross (see plates), and this award usually came with a promotion, he cannot have been promoted to *Gefreiter* because he already was one. The inevitable conclusion is that his promotion must have been from *Gefreiter* to *Obergefreiter*. The double chevron insignia of the rank of *Obergefreiter* can be seen at the bottom left of the display of Hetzenauer's awards in the plates. This is physical evidence that he was indeed promoted to *Obergefreiter* in the last few weeks of his service. The rank of *Obergefreiter* was roughly equivalent to lance-corporal in the British Army but lacked NCO status.

Hetzenauer's Decorations

Very probably, Hetzenauer was the most decorated of all Wehrmacht non-NCOs. As at mid-March 1945 the regimental official record, included in the recommendation for the Knight's Cross and featured in the plates of this book, shows the following awards and decorations for Hetzenauer:

(i) Iron Cross Second Class. (Awarded to compensate for the cancellation of his hits prior to 1 September 1944).

(ii) Black Wound Badge. (Awarded for shrapnel wound to the head, 9 November 1944, three days earlier. The Wound Badge second item down, left side on his display of awards, is not black, but probably silver or gold, and therefore to receive this badge Hetzenauer was wounded a second or third time in the last two months of the war.

(iii) Infantry Assault Badge in Silver. (Awarded 13 November 1944, item top left of display.)

(iv) Iron Cross First Class. (Awarded 25 November 1944.)

(v) Sniper Badge in Gold. (Awarded 3 December 1944)

(vi) Knight's Cross of the Iron Cross. (Awarded 17 April 1945)

(vii) Close Combat Bar in Gold. (Awarded on or before 17 April 1945. This decoration appears upside down in the right-hand column of the display above the Edelweiss badge. In the photograph in the plates of the award ceremony to Hetzenauer of the Knight's Cross, he is seen wearing the Close Combat Bar above the left pocket of his tunic, and this award was therefore likely made on a date between 16 March 1945 and 17 April 1945.

(viii) German Cross in Gold. (Seen in Hetzenauer's display immediately above the Close Combat Bar in Gold. Awarded jointly with the Close Combat Bar in Gold.) On 30 August 1944, Hitler ordered that the German Cross in Gold could be awarded to the wearers of the Close Combat Bar in Gold without any further recommendation since they had proved their bravery repeatedly by the number of days they had spent in close combat. See Rolf Michaels, *Deutsche Kriegsauszeichnungen 1939–1945, Heer – Waffen-SS – Polizei*, p. 29.

Introduction

The Origins and Lebensraum *of the Hetzenauers*

BESIDES THE MEANING commonly understood nowadays, *Lebensraum* is the native environment of the family into which a person is born and the place impregnated with its stamp from centuries past. Despite the levelling effects of modern mass tourism, big city and industrial influences, there have always been and always will be close relationships between people and their home areas, so that a person is a 'product' of their history. That applies especially to tradition-conscious Tyroleans. If you wish to know and understand them better, you must come to terms with their historical development. If you try to analyse the character of the Tyrolean, one thing must be borne constantly in mind: even if they say they are progressive, in their way of thinking and living they are primarily conservative. The word 'conservative' here has the sense of the classical Latin *conservare*, meaning to preserve and uphold and refers to the old virtues. The conservatism of the Tyrolean is rural in nature.

The region of the Tyrol where Matthäus Hetzenauer spent his life when not in military service or captivity is the mountainous area near Kitzbühel, bordered on the north by Bavaria, and to the east by Berchtesgaden. The main Austrian centre of population and administration nearby is Salzburg. The roots of the Tyrolean people are without doubt to be found in the long-ago Celtic era. Europe's Hallstatt culture of the early Iron Age at the end of the eighth century BCE to the termination of the Celtic expansion in the fifth and fourth centuries BCE takes its name from a village

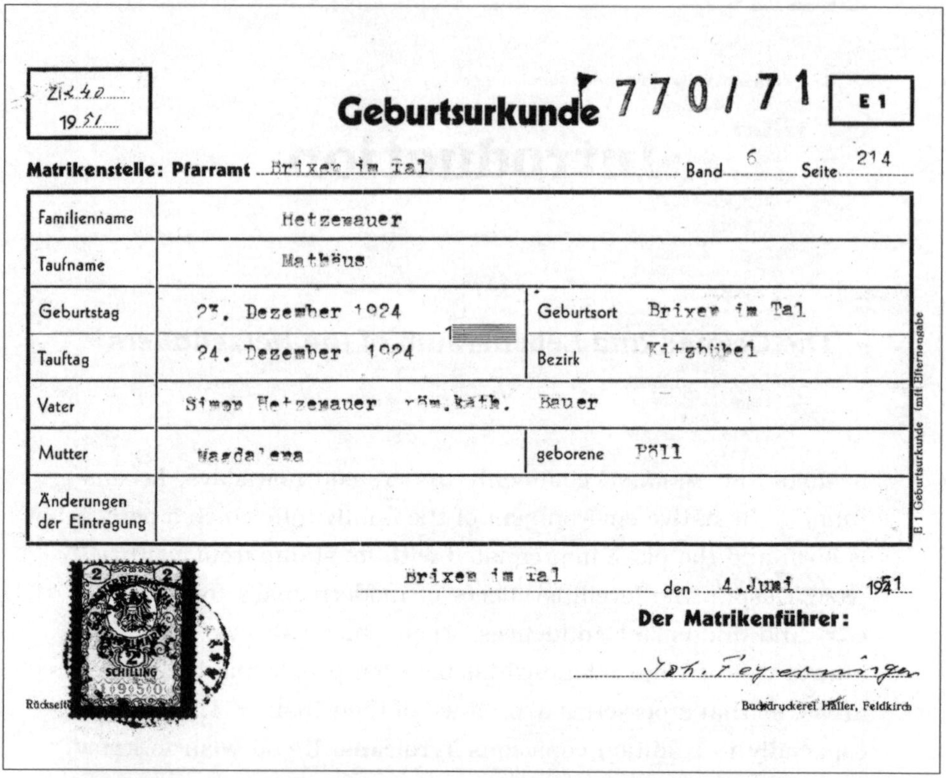

Zi. 40
19 51

Geburtsurkunde 770/71 **E 1**

Matrikenstelle: Pfarramt Brixen im Tal Band 6 Seite 214

Familienname	Hetzenauer		
Taufname	Mathäus		
Geburtstag	23. Dezember 1924	Geburtsort	Brixen im Tal
Tauftag	24. Dezember 1924 1[redacted]	Bezirk	Kitzbühel
Vater	Simon Hetzenauer röm.kath.	Bauer	
Mutter	Magdalena	geborene	Pöll
Änderungen der Eintragung			

E 1 Geburtsurkunde (mit Elternangabe)

Brixen im Tal den 4. Juni 1951

Der Matrikenführer:

Joh. Feyersinger

2 SCHILLING

Rückseit…

Buchdruckerei Haller, Feldkirch

Authenticated copy birth certificate made in 1951 from the ecclesiastical register for 'Mathäus' Hetzenauer ('Mathäus' is presumably a typographical error). His place of birth is given as Brixen im Tal, as it was known in 1924.

in this region.[1] It was succeeded by the Celtic La Tène culture,[2] which developed around 500 BCE and whose core region extended from the River Seine to Bohemia, from the Lower Rhine to the Austrian Alps.

The Celts and Romans were aware of the wonders of the Brixental climate. Around the year 1800, Brixen im Thale, as it is correctly written, was known above all as a health spa which along

1. Hallstatt, a modern tourist centre, is situated at the foot of mountains on the shore of the lake of that name located between Salzburg and Graz. The Kitzbühel area was within the core of the Celtic development.
2. A term used by archaeologists for the later period of art and culture of the ancient Celts, derived from the site at La Tène on the north shore of Lake Neuchâtel in Switzerland.

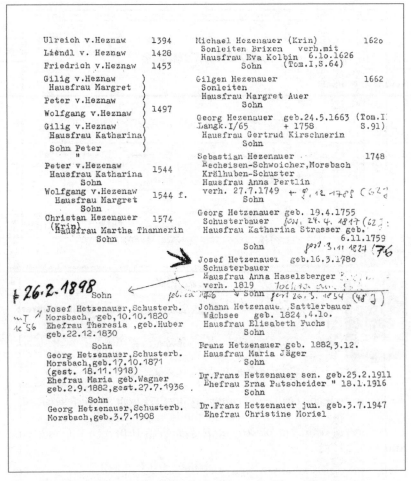

Ulreich v.Heznaw 1394
Liendl v. Heznaw 1428
Friedrich v.Heznaw 1453
Gilig v.Heznaw
Hausfrau Margret
Peter v.Heznaw
Wolfgang v.Heznaw } 1497
Gilig v.Heznaw
Hausfrau Katharina
Sohn Peter
"
Peter v.Hezenaw 1544
Hausfrau Katharina
Sohn
Wolfgang v.Hezenaw 1544 f.
Hausfrau Margret
Sohn
Christan Hezenauer 1574
(Krin)
Hausfrau Martha Thannerin
Sohn

Michael Hezenauer (Krin) 1620
Sonleiten Brixen verh.mit
Hausfrau Eva Kolbin 6.10.1626
Sohn (Tom.I,S.64)

Gilgen Hezenauer 1662
Sonleiten
Hausfrau Margret Auer
Sohn

Georg Hezenauer geb.24.5.1663 (Tom.I:
Langk.I/65 + 1758 S.91)
Hausfrau Gertrud Kirschnerin
Sohn

Sebastian Hezenauer 1748
Recheisen-Schwoicher,Morsbach
Krälhuben-Schuster
Hausfrau Anna Pertlin
verh. 27.7.1749
Sohn

Georg Hetzenauer geb. 19.4.1755
Schusterbauer
Hausfrau Katharina Strasser geb.
6.11.1759
Sohn

Josef Hetzenauer geb.16.3.1780
Schusterbauer
Hausfrau Anna Haselsberger
verh. 1819
Sohn

† 26.2.1898
Sohn

Josef Hetzenauer,Schusterb.
Morsbach, geb,10.10.1820
Ehefrau Theresia ,geb.Huber
geb.22.12.1830
Sohn
Georg Hetzenauer,Schusterb.
Morsbach,geb.17.10.1871
(gest. 18.11.1918)
Ehefrau Maria geb.Wagner
geb.2.9.1882,gest.27.7.1936
Sohn
Georg Hetzenauer,Schusterb.
Morsbach,geb.3.7.1908

Johann Hetzenauer ,Sattlerbauer
Wachsee geb. 1824 ,4.10.
Hausfrau Elisabeth Fuchs
Sohn
Franz Hetzenauer geb. 1882,3.12.
Hausfrau Maria Jäger
Sohn
Dr.Franz Hetzenauer sen. geb.25.2.1911
Ehefrau Erna Putscheider " 18.1.1916
Sohn
Dr.Franz Hetzenauer jun. geb.3.7.1947
Ehefrau Christine Moriel

The ancestral table drawn up by the historian Dr Franz Hetzenauer stretches back to the fourteenth century.

with neighbouring Kitzbühel was visited by many personalities of rank and substance.

The Hetzenauers are to a man the descendants of ancient peasant stock in the Tyrolean community of Kirchberg. The ancestral village Hetzenau (today Hetzober) is in the Spertental along the valley on a height to the left of Aschau. In the year 902 CE the Regensburg prince-bishopric (*Hochstift*) obtained Brixental with everything which the valley possessed in people and territory by means of a Bavarian donation. In 1133 this prince-

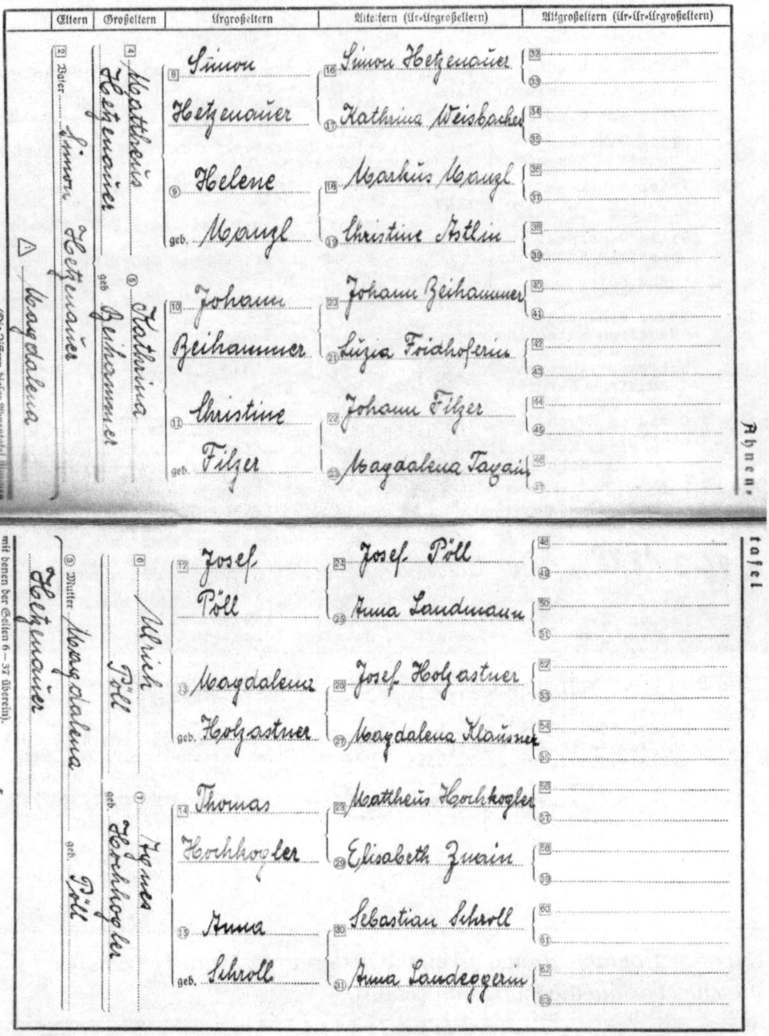

This genealogical tree was drafted for Magdalena Hetzenauer, sister of Matthäus, and is traced back to their great-great-grandparents.

bishopric is recorded as owner of the county (*Grafschaft*) in the Inn valley, which probably stretched from the mouth of the Ziller via Nussdorf am Inn downstream on the right bank of the river.[1] Regensburg may therefore also have possessed the fief of Heznaw. Regensburg's Bishop Albert I of Pietengau (1247–59) pledged the

1. Janner, Ferdinands, *Geschichte der Bischöfe von Regensburg*, Vol. 2, p. 42.

The Itter mountain crest overlooking the Brixen valley entrance.

At the end of the war, Schloss Itter was being used by the Nazis as a prison for Prominente, *distinguished enemy prisoners.*

properties of the bishopric in the Lower Inn Valley parishes of Söll, Kelschau and Brixen to the nobleman Gebhard von Velben, who had other holdings in Brixental. As with all ancient villages of the time, the village and family names sounded the same.

In 1394 the name of Ulreich von Heznaw appeared as witness in a contract by which a fief at Windau was sold to the ecclesiastical provost at Kirchberg in Tyrol.

On 2 May 1428 the Prince-Archbishop Eberhard von Salzburg invested Liendl von Heznaw at Itter with 'a half of the Heznaw estate in the Sperten[tal]'. Following the imposition of the Reich tax in *Pfennigs*, the so-called 'Turkish tax' of 1497, the document shows that at Brixental, Gilig (wife Katharina), Gilig (wife Margret), Peter and Wolfgang, all of the surname von Heznaw, each owned a quarter part of Heznaw.

In 1574 Peter Hezenauer took over Hezenaw and Christian (or Christan) Hezenauer became a landowner at Krin am Krinberg in the Spertental by marrying Martha Thanner in the same year. Their marriage bore four children, one of whom, Michael Hezenauer, married Eva Kolbin zu Sonleiten, this last being a village above Brixen im Thale, on 6 October 1626. The Hezenauer couple gave this property to their own son, Gilgen Hezenauer, on 15 February 1662.

The genealogical tree then traces this branch of the ancestral line so far as is possible until Franz Xaver Hetzenauer was born as the seventh child of eleven siblings on 3 December 1882. His son was the historian Dr Franz Hetzenauer Sr.[1]

On 23 December 1924, Matthäus Hetzenauer was born as the son of Sonnleit farmer Simon Hetzenauer and his wife Magdalena (*née* Pöll) at Brixen im Thale. The village forms the geographical, historical and cultural centrepoint of the approximately 25-kilometre long Brixental, which is a side valley of the main Inn Valley originating at Wörgl and then stretching eastwards over the Itter mountain crest with its military prohibited area and Schloss Itter, through Hopfgarten, Westerndorf and Kirchberg to the world-famous ski paradise of Kitzbühel.

1. Hetzenauer, Franz, *Das Geschichte der Hetzenauer* (manuscript).

The Hetzenauers' Sonnleithof farmhouse in the Kitzbühel Alps.

The centre of the village of Brixen im Thale is dominated by the twin towers of the parish and deanery church whose beginnings go back to the Holy Roman Empire. It was later rebuilt in baroque style, and then renewed in the classical style after serious structural damage.

On Christmas Eve 1924 the one-day-old Matthäus was baptised here as a Roman Catholic. The baptismal font, positioned at the right-hand side as one enters the church, is surmounted by the sculpted figure of an angel in the form of a baby sleeping against a human skull. What that is intended to signify is not clear. He had two brothers and one sister, and in his happy childhood on the Sonnleithof was a busy farmhand. He attended the numerous religious festivals and observances of the parish church at Brixen im Thale, in those days remote and untouched by mass tourism.

In Tyrol the piety of the people goes hand-in-hand with the joy of living. The population is overwhelmingly Roman Catholic,

Simon Hetzenauer, father of the sniper, as a hunter.

Magdalena Hetzenauer, mother of the sniper, at her spinning wheel.

Hunting trophies at the Hetzenauer house.

The parish church of the Ascension of the Virgin Mary at Brixen im Thale.

The baptismal font with the sleeping angel and death's head at the entrance to the parish church.

although recently secularisation and the liberalisation of creeds have contributed to the growth of local evangelical Christianity.

The marked religious observation and piety of the Tyroleans is seen in many areas of life. Most customs and usages are rooted in it, for example *Walpurgisnacht* (celebrated on 30 April), the *Wallfahrten* (pilgrimages to churches or other places of religious significance), *Leonhardiritte* and *Georgenritte* (mounted processions wearing traditional costume), the Thiersee and Erler Passion Plays and *Fronleichnamstag* (Feast of the Most Holy Body and Blood of Christ) on a day between 21 May and 24 June. These and others are fixed components of the old customs in the Lower Inn Valley.

These traditions and ancient values are held in special regard in the Brixental. Thus for centuries farmers have made the ride to the Schweden-kapelle on *Fronleichnamstag* to repeat their thanksgiving that the valley was not plundered during the Thirty Years War. The huntsmen, musical bands and national dress societies also have a long tradition.

The world-famous winter-sports resort of Kitzbühel at the end of the Brixen valley.

Kitzbühel and the Kitzbühel Alps where skiing competitions are held, including races on the spectacular Hahnenkamm course.

Brixen im Thale, birthplace of Matthäus Hetzenauer, against the backdrop of the Kitzbühel Alps.

The inhabitants of the Brixental celebrate their festivals in baroque style. The picturesque Tyrolean traditional dress, based to a large extent on that of the courtly Baroque period, is proudly worn, especially on Church feast days and public holidays. The costly garments will not infrequently have made their way down through several generations.

Customs such as the carrying of a palm frond on Palm Sunday, *Pfingstschiessen* (Whitsun archery), *Kräuterbüschel* (binding weeds for the celebration on 15 August of the Ascension of the Virgin Mary) and the Holy Day celebration itself, Harvest Thanksgiving on the first Sunday in October, *Herbergsuchen* (ceremony of Christmas visiting), *Weihnachts-schiessen* (Christmas skeet or marksmanship competitions) and singing under the stars between New Year's Eve and Twelfth Night, continue to be a living tradition in the 'Holy Land' of Tyrol, closely bound to the Church year.

Josef Hetzenauer, brother of sniper Matthäus Hetzenauer, at the Fronleichnam procession.

Bishop Madersbacher leading the Fronleichnam procession. Holding the flag is Matthäus Hetzenauer's son Hermann.

A herd of deer in the Kitzbühel Alps above Aurach graze the lush grasses.

The well-known Tyrolean custom, also celebrated in the Brixental, of blowing the alpine horn.

The fork in the road which the visitor takes to the Sonnleithof.

The comprehensive collection of Hetzenauer trophies . . .

. . . even includes a stuffed mountain cock or wood grouse.

Farmer and Huntsman in the Kitzbühel Alps

The by no means mild climate of the Austrian Tyrol, which demands of its inhabitants such strength, endurance and toughness, is determined by the situation at the northern edge of the mighty Alps. The best known climatic phenomenon of Tyrol – and of the entire northern edge of the Alps – is the wind called the *Föhn*. Our forebears did not quite understand it and thought that mild air from hot Africa had strayed to the raw northern alpine landscape. Today we know better. The *Föhn* is a warm, dry katabatic wind which, as it passes over the main crest of the Alps coming up from the Mediterranean, is cooled on the alpine southern side to cause precipitation on the inclined slopes, while on the alpine northern side it is dry – adiabatic – therefore strongly warmed and so falls into the valley as a warm, dry wind.

After he left elementary school, there began for Matthäus Hetzenauer a life of hard work and privation on the family farm. The property is situated above the Brixental on the northern slopes of the Kitzbühel Alps in sight of the Hohe Salve. It is at the centre of a mountain world in which the charming villages of Kirchberg, Brixen im Thale and Westerndorf, and the side valleys running to the south, offer magnificent natural landscapes rarely to be matched anywhere.

The variety of the mountain formations in the Kitzbühel Alps is remarkable. Soft grassy mountains preponderate and are treasured by hikers. Alpine huts and hunting lodges offer food and lodging to fortify the climber. The Kitzbühel Alps are numbered amongst the Tyrolean and adjoining Bavarian regions most rich in wild life. It is no wonder that hunters and poachers – now mostly motorised – have such a long tradition here.

On 6 November 1877, 29-year-old poacher Georg 'Girgl' Jennerwein was shot dead by a game warden on the Peissenberg heights, Tegernsee. His memory is still preserved today in the alpine territories. Old shooting targets picturing Jennerwein's end hang in inns, hunting lodges and alpine huts and make their own contribution to the glorification and romance of the hunter/poacher.

Pictures celebrating the WWI service of Josef Hetzenauer, uncle of the sniper.

Gebetsandenken
an Se. Apostolische Majestät
Franz Josef I.
Kaiser von Oesterreich, König von Ungarn, Böhmen etc.

geboren zu Schönbrunn bei Wien am 18. August 1830; trat nach der Thronentsagung Kaisers Ferdinand und der Thronfolge-Verzichtleistung seines Vaters am 2. Dezember 1848 die Regierung an; wurde am 8. Juni 1867 zum König von Ungarn gekrönt; vermählt am 24. April 1854 mit Kaiserin Elisabeth [durch Mörderhand gestorben 10. Sept. 1898]; feierte das 60jähr. Regierungsjubiläum 1908; starb nach 68jähr. Regierung zu Schönbrunn, versehen mit den hl. Sterbesakramenten, am 21. Nov. 1916.

Ein Fürstenherz, schwer geprüft wie keines, das sich verzehrte in Liebe und Arbeit für das Wohl seiner treuen Völker, und das im Glauben und in der Ergebung in Gottes Willen seinen Trost fand in den herbsten Prüfungen, hat ausgeschlagen. Die Majestät des Todes hat die dornenumrankte Herrscherkrone dem greisen Monarchen abgenommen. Weinend stehen Oesterreichs Völker an der Bahre „Franz Josef des Gütigen", den sie nimmer vergessen werden.

Herr, gib deinem Diener Franz Josef die ewige Ruhe, und das ewige Licht leuchte ihm. Herr, lasse ihn ruhen im Frieden. Amen. — Vater unser.

Prayer Card kept by the Hetzenauers in remembrance of Franz Josef I, Emperor of Austria.

The savage romanticism of the hunter/poacher. An armed game warden catches a poacher in the act.

The collection of First World War decorations awarded to Josef Hetzenauer.

A Tyrolean hunter in full hunting dress,armed with a hunting rifle.

The memorial to the noted poacher Georg Jennerwein at Schliersee.

Hermann, son of Matthäus Hetzenauer, with a fourteen-pointer.

The massive expansion of forest paths into the high mountain regions has given the poacher fresh assistance. A calf may now be transported by livestock waggon in a night operation from its summery pasture to some remote alpine lodge or inn where for a week or so roast venison will be replaced by veal cutlets prepared in all imaginable creations *a là Wienerschnitzel*.

Chapter 1

Gebirgsjäger Training at Kufstein

HAD THE TIMES BEEN DIFFERENT, Hetzenauer would probably have followed a settled existence as a mountain farmer and hunter in the charming Brixental in the wild, romantic mountain world of the Kitzbühel Alps. Instead he was torn from the everyday life of the farmer by the fury of war and forced to wear the field grey uniform of the German Wehrmacht – not just any uniform, but that of the mountain troops of the *Gebirgsjäger*. In September 1942 at the age of seventeen years and nine months he was conscripted into 140th Mountain Rifle Reinforcement Battalion at Kufstein.

In 1936 work had begun in that Tyrolean fortress town on a barracks, with two buildings for recruits and one for the domestic offices. After Austria was annexed into the German *Reich*, the barracks was expanded. On 6 April 1938 at Innsbruck, 6th Division, Austrian Army of the First Republic, under Generalmajor Valentin Feurstein, was converted into 2nd Mountain Division, German Army, attached to Salzburg Military District XVIII with local offices at Bludenz, Landeck, Imst, Innsbruck, Hall in Tirol, Schwaz, Wörgl, Kufstein, Salzburg, Saalfelden, Zell am See, St Johann, Radstadt, Lienz and Spital an der Drau.

The 2nd Battalion, 140th Mountain Rifle Regiment, came into being at the former peacetime local depots in Kufstein and Wörgl. In 1938 it was part of the Tyrolean Infantry Regiment, but at the outbreak of war was attached to 136th Mountain Rifle Regiment at Innsbruck, and later transformed into its 2nd Battalion there.

Matthäus Hetzenauer did his basic training as a *Gebirgsjäger* at Kufstein, both on the parade ground and in the alpine environment

The Steinberg training area on the Wilder Kaiser not far from Brixen im Thale.

Starting point for climbing tours was Hinterbärenbad amidst the rocky giants of the Wild Kaiser such as Totensessel and Ellmauer Halt.

Honour salute at the burial of a soldier who died in an accident at Hinterthiersee/Kufstein on 4 March 1939.

of the Wilder Kaiser. The training period presented no difficulties for the hardened son of a mountain farmer who had had to do his share on the land even in his very young years, and who as a boy had learned to be at home in the raw mountains.

The training of mountain soldiers takes more time than for those on the flat. In the matter of health protection alone, the increasing physical and mental demands made of a young man in mountain service require a certain period of preparation. An established mastery of basic techniques on the plain is a precondition for the difficulties of service in the mountains. The training of mountain troops can be simplified, however, if only those men who have grown up in the mountains and are therefore familiar with their special demands are accepted into that branch of service.

In the course of time there crystallised in every mountain unit – from company to battalion – a small mountain-climber elite especially suited for difficult assignments in the high uplands. In creating this elite within its pre-Hitler 100,000-man force

Front cover of a RAD pass for a young woman.

Magdalena Hetzenauer, the sniper's sister, on her RAD documents.

Troops of the Wehrmacht entering the Tyrolean fortress town of Kufstein.

The Kaindl Lodge in the foothills of the Scheffauer was a starting point for mountain training by the Kufstein Gebirgsjäger-Bataillon *in the Wilder Kaiser.*

imposed by the Treaty of Versailles, the German Army had made great strides with its so-called Army Mountain Leader Training (*Heeresbergführerausbildung*). When the necessity arose later, this made it much easier to put together an alpine leadership by setting up *Hochgebirgsjäger* battalions. These units then went through a uniform training at a high mountain-climber level which aimed at great alpine achievements for definite military purposes. For the active officers and NCOs and suitable younger reserve officers of the *Gebirgsjäger*, annual summer and winter courses in high-mountain training were introduced. The rest were only trained up to 'medium-difficult' mountain standard with full kit, taught how to avoid vertigo and to dress for the conditions.

Transforming a lowland division into one having capability in mountains of medium height – including training in handling mules – and revising battle training required weeks. According to the size of the squad, the mules caused the greatest problems. Therefore the overall adaptation period and then the completion of battle training needed considerably more time. With the right kind of direction and leadership, these lesser mountain divisions would be able to carry out assignments in terrain corresponding to their ability, but it would be wrong to think that any number of mountain divisions could be created simply by adapting lowland divisions. In the mountains, only those can endure who have had a thorough instruction. The German Wehrmacht trained its mountain soldiers bearing this fact in mind.

The *Gebirgsjäger* received thorough further instruction at the *Gebirgsjäger* school, Mittenwald, the *Hochgebirgsjäger* school in the Tyrolean Stubaital and the Army NCOs' school for *Gebirgsjäger* at Wörgl.

The mountain march is an important preparatory exercise for military training in the mountains. Carrying rucksack and rifle on one's back it is anything but a pleasant excursion into the mountain world. Even in difficult going, order must always be maintained in the column and formation. Above all, taking short cuts on one's own initiative is forbidden. Thus a march in the mountains imposes a heavy physical and mental burden on the participants, the climatic conditions prevailing in the peaks more so. The young mountain soldier must first of all become familiarised with the special conditions in the mountains. For this reason mountain marches have a special significance.

> The purpose of march training is not to discourage young soldiers but to inspire them. Asking too much of soldiers at the beginning of training is to be avoided under all circumstances. The demands of mountain marches have a purpose and are to be constantly increased. The required will and preparedness to better oneself on every mountain march come from within when the soldier does not return 'sour' after his first mountain march but proud of his achievement.
>
> On this march only the absolutely necessary kit (rations and suitable clothing for cold and wet conditions)

German Army troops crossing the German–Austrian border at Kiefersfelden on the road to Kufstein in March 1938. In the background is the neo-Gothic Otto chapel.

> is required, and only personal weapons should be carried. In general on the familiarisation march a height gain of one thousand metres is to be achieved at about three hundred metres ascent per hour. The entire march should not last longer than eight hours.[1]

Later the effort was to be increased. The marches were to be longer and more difficult, the equipment equivalent to that used in action and the height to be overcome greater. After basic training at Kufstein and in the surrounding mountains Matthäus Hetzenauer was given his discharge and returned to his parents' farm, Sonnleithof at Brixental. This was only for a short while, for in January 1943 he was re-conscripted. Between 27 March and 1 June 1943, first he completed basic training on the medium mortar. During this period and until the end of June 1943 he was stationed at the following depots:

1. *Wehrausbildung in Wort und Bild*, 1969, Vol. 7, p. 299.

The Tyrolean fortress town of Kufstein was supposedly a bastion of the mythical 'Alpine Redoubt' at the end of the war in 1945. In the foreground is the bridge over the River Inn.

Report, 1 April 1943

1st Permanent Staff Company, 2nd Battalion, 137th Mountain Rifle Reserve and Training Regiment

Report, 5 and 6 April 1943

To 10th Company, Reserve and Training Battalion, 137th Mountain Rifle Reserve and Training Regiment

Report 6 June 1943

To Permanent Staff Company, 2nd Battalion, 137th Mountain Rifle Reserve and Training Regiment

Report 18 June 1943

To 18th National Rifleman Reserve and Training Battalion at Lienz

Report 20 June 1943
From 1st Training Company, Lienz, to 4th Home Company at Lienz
Report 25 June 1943
To 3rd Company at Lienz
Report 29 June 1943
To 4th Company at Lienz

(ID disc: -5718-. 1. Stamm.Kp. II. Ers.Btl./Geb.Jg.Ers. Rgt. 137)

From 2 July 1943 to 26 March 1944 Hetzenauer was returned by the Military Reporting Office (*Wehrmeldeamt*) Kufstein to 4th Permanent Staff Company at Lienz as above.

Chapter 2

Sniper Training in the Seetaler Alps

BETWEEN 27 MARCH AND 16 JULY 1944 Matthäus Hetzenauer was sent for training in marksmanship to the Styrian troop depot in the Seetaler Alps where he was issued immediately with a Karabiner 98k. This weapon, known officially as the Mauser Model 98, was a version of the most important German military rifle manufactured from 1898. With a shortened barrel, the Model 98 became the 98k carbine and for long years served as the standard rifle of the German Army. Its effective breech mechanism made the Mauser carbine one of the most-produced weapons in the world.[1]

As a passionate hunter with a trained eagle eye Hetzenauer was pre-destined for sniper training. The journey to the Seetaler Alps seemed like a great undertaking for a farmhand who up to then had been tied to his parent's house at the remote Sonnleithof and who until then had never been out of the narrow confines of the Kitzbühel region. To get to green Styria (or Steiermark as it is known to the Austrians) where he had never set foot before and which he only knew through the writings of the great Styrian poet Peter Rosegger von der Waldheimat, he boarded a train to take him east from Kufstein via Salzburg and across the Salzkammergut to the Styrian provincial capital, Graz.

From there he went via Köflach and the Stubalpe in the direction of Judenburg at the north-eastern exits of the Seetaler Alps. The name Seetal comes from the numerous small and large lakes strewn across the landscape of this mountain region. A mountain

1. Law, Richard D., *Karabiner 98k, 1934–1945*, and *Scharfschützenwaffen*, Stuttgart 2012.

Visitors to the small town of Obdach at the south-eastern entrance to the Seetaler Alps training depot see friendly arrival and departure messages.

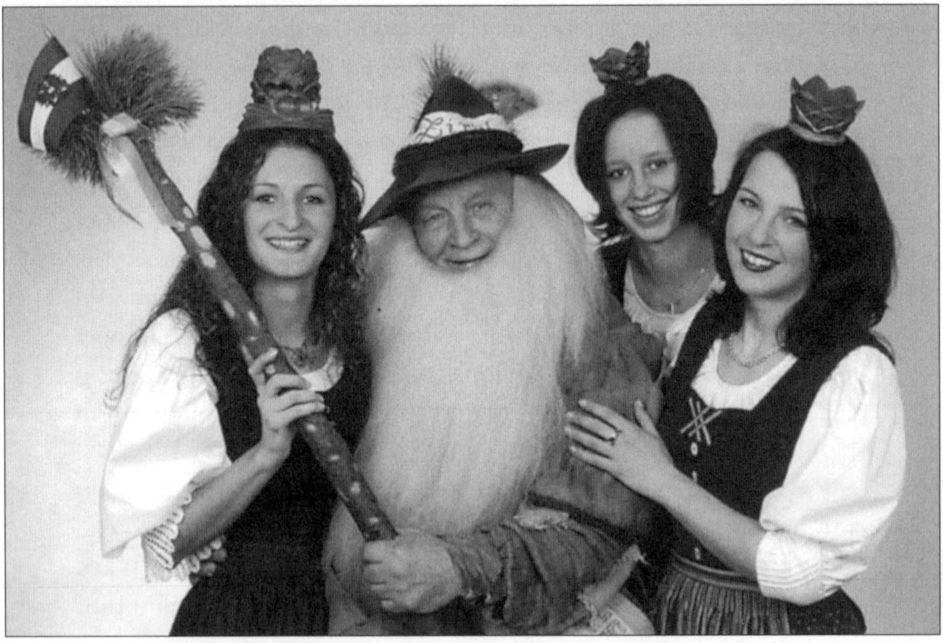

The Pine Queen with her two Pine Princesses and the bearded Zirbl represent the pinelands of Steiermark

Entfernungen von Hohen Ranach

FAN	1700m	Scharfes Eck	4700m
Speikkogel	1900m	PAR Felsen	1900m
Speikplateau	1670m	Panzerscheibenzuganlage	1170m
Checkpoint	1250m	Sprengplatz Seetal	1030m
Sprengplatz Erlenboden	2060m	Panzerwrack	1000m
Frauenlacke	1560m	Schusterleiten	2300m
Zirbitzkogel	5550m	Kreiskogel	3160m

This panorama of the surrounding mountains from the Hohe Ranach gives an idea of the landscape of the Seetaler Alps.

Overleaf: *A present-day map of the Seetaler Alps Troop-Training Depot.*

Key: *Sperrgebietsgrenze: Borders of Prohibited Zone*
vom Sperrgebiet ausgenommene Wanderwege: Hiking paths exempted from the Prohibited Zone
Weitwanderwege: Long distance hiking paths

Truppenübungs

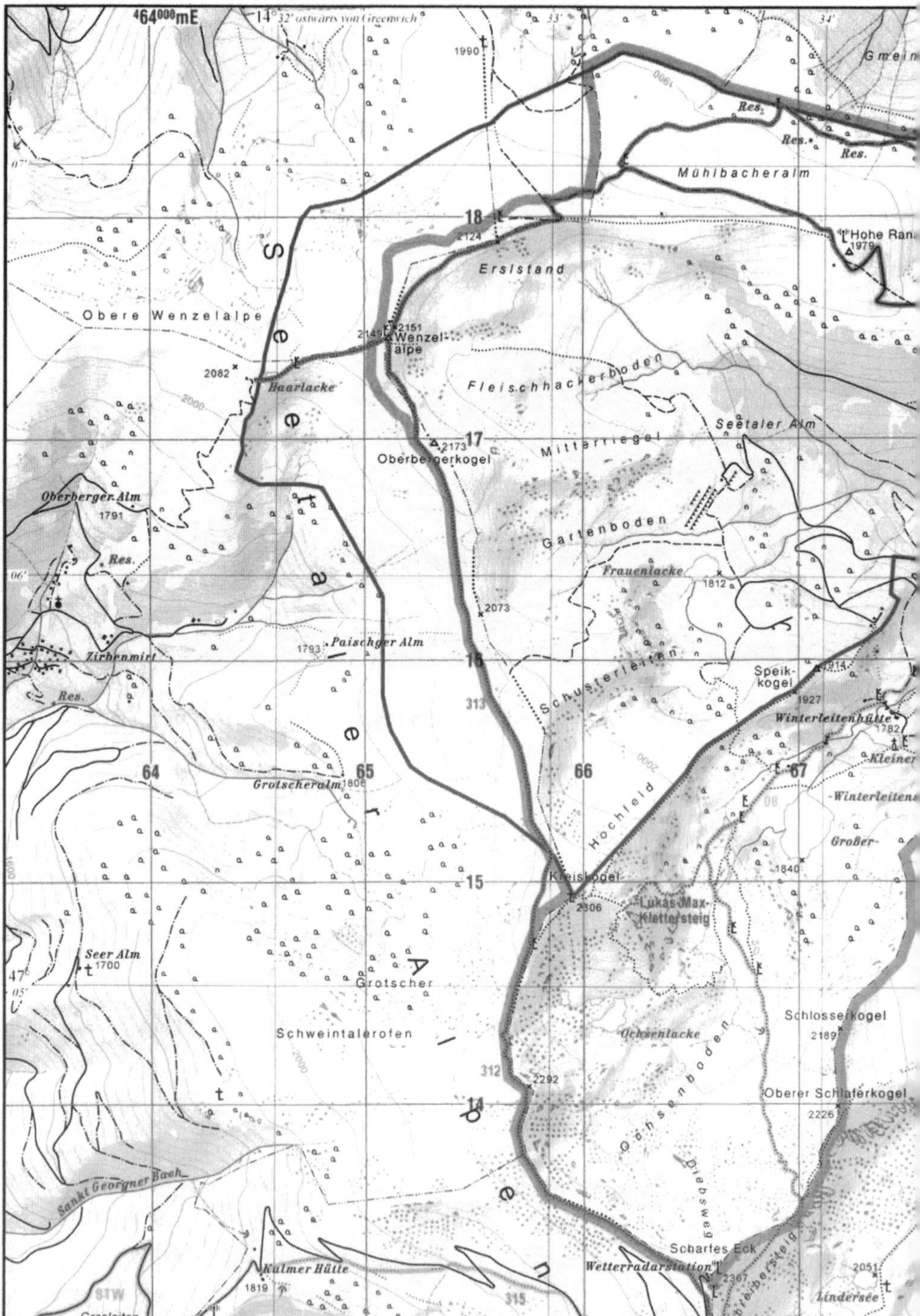

tz Seetaler Alpe

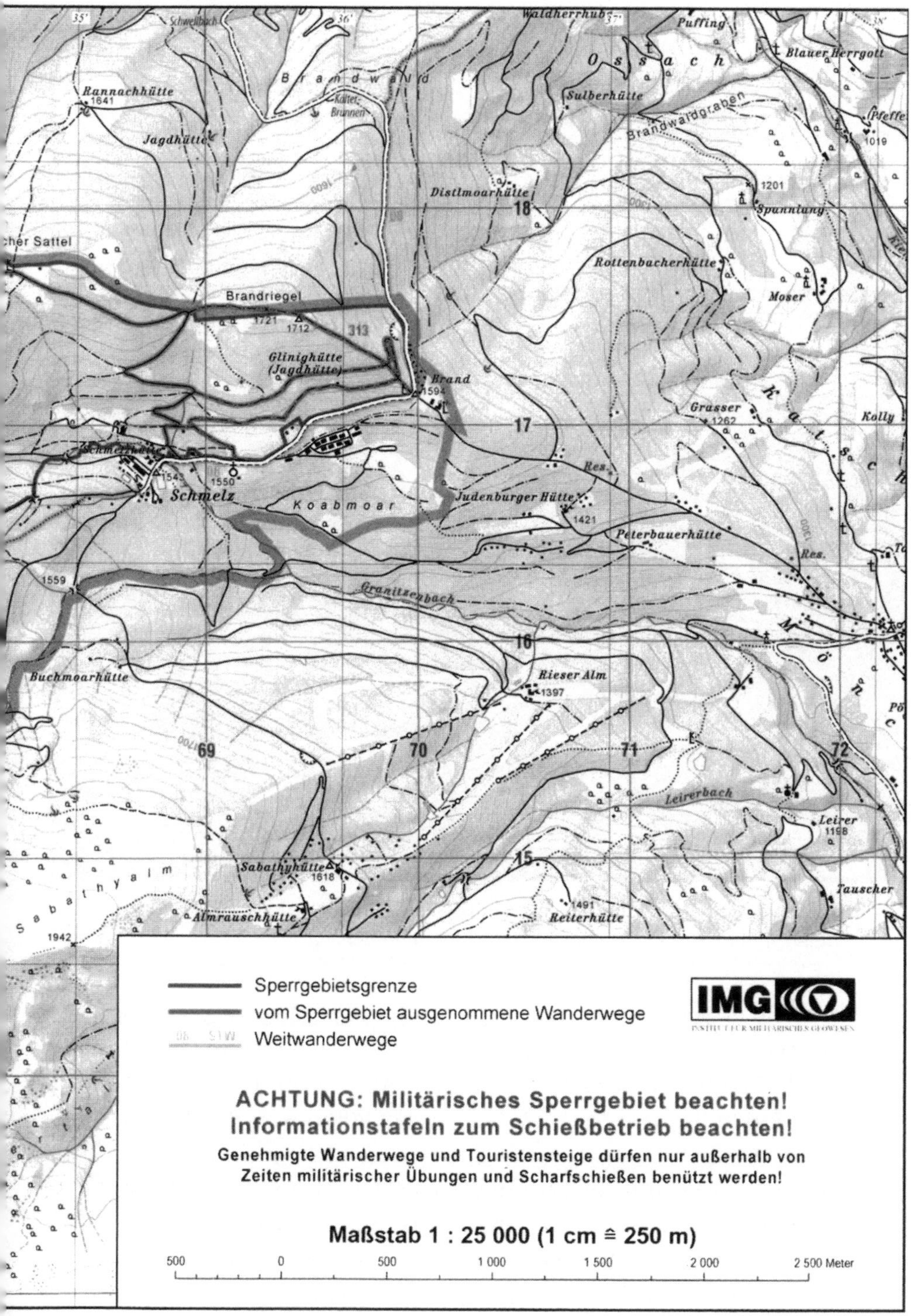

View of the Seetaler Alps Troop-Training Depot. As well as the various military installations, the facilities include a tennis court.

road takes the traveller into the mountains at Mönchegg and St Wolfgang, the only large villages near the troop-training depot, overlooked to the north by the Wenzel Alpe (2,149 metres/7,051 feet) and to the west by the Zirbitzkogel (2,396 metres/7,861 feet). Sleepy Obdach in the heart of Zirbenland, Steiermark province, serves as the south-eastern entrance to the troop-training depot.

In 1938 and 1939, after the annexation of Austria into the German Reich, the German Settlement Society – a central office for Wehrmacht affairs – purchased 5,140 hectares (12,700 acres) of land in the Seetaler Alps for the troop-training depot. The lodges at Schmelz, Winterleiten and Sabathy were also bought up for military use.

The German Wehrmacht now began extensive building work with barracks for accommodation, offices and general house-keeping to take 1,200 men, stables, the command building, officers' quarters, a forestry barrack, a shower block, officers' mess, workshops, telephone exchange, an electrical power station on the Schmelzbach and a stone-crusher installation for gravel. In 1940 and 1941 a cable-car system for materials was set up from Strettweg near Judenburg via an intermediate station at Reiterbauer to Schmelz with the former stables as the head station. The technical details are of interest:

7,384 metres	Total length
4,312 metres	Strettweg to Reiterbauer
3,072 metres	Reiterbauer to Schmelz
850 metres	Overall difference in altitude

Marksmanship training was held in the nearby troop depots of Stablack, Hohenfels, Obergruppe, Wandern, Lamsdorf and Münsingen. The best-known of these with the highest reputation was the troop-training depot in the Seetaler Alps where the best marksmen of the German Wehrmacht from all Second World War fronts came either to train as snipers or – if they had already been deployed at the front in this role – for further training.

Snipers are true masters of patience who, if you will, have a long tradition to which they can look back, for in the times before the introduction of firearms specially trained soldiers, for example archers, were deployed as lone warriors for their accuracy.[1] Outstanding vision, faculty for observation and a sharp eye are the hallmarks and indispensable preconditions of the sniper. What he also needs in order to meet the demands of his assignments is, as mentioned elsewhere, patience, a virtue the sniper cannot do without. This applies as much to the encounter itself as when he lies in wait to a certain extent like a hunter. 'The

1. Farey, Pat, & Spicer, Mark, *Scharfschützen, Meister der Geduld*, Stuttgart, 2010.

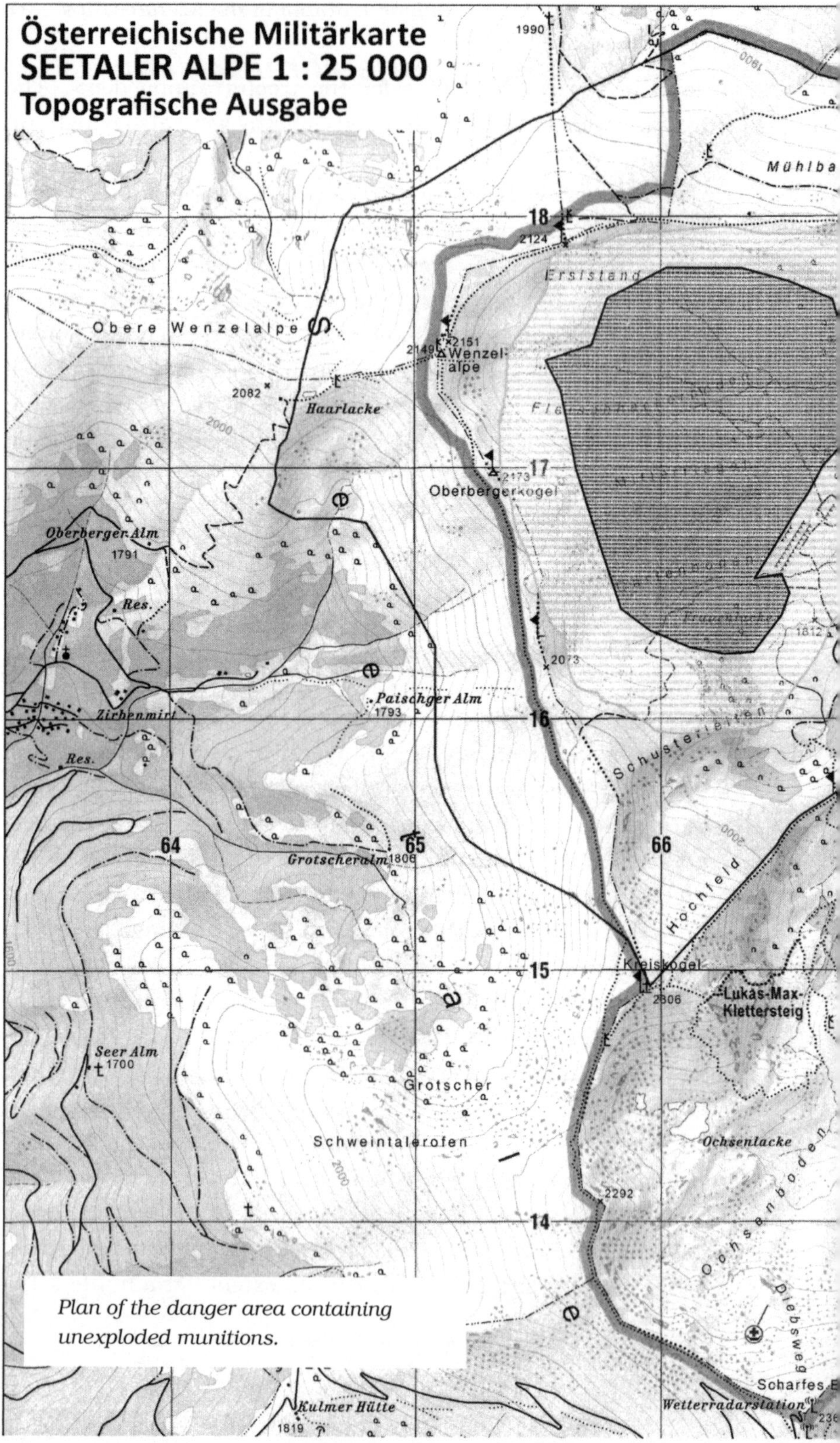

Plan of the danger area containing unexploded munitions.

Blindgängergefahrenzonenplan mit 12 04 11

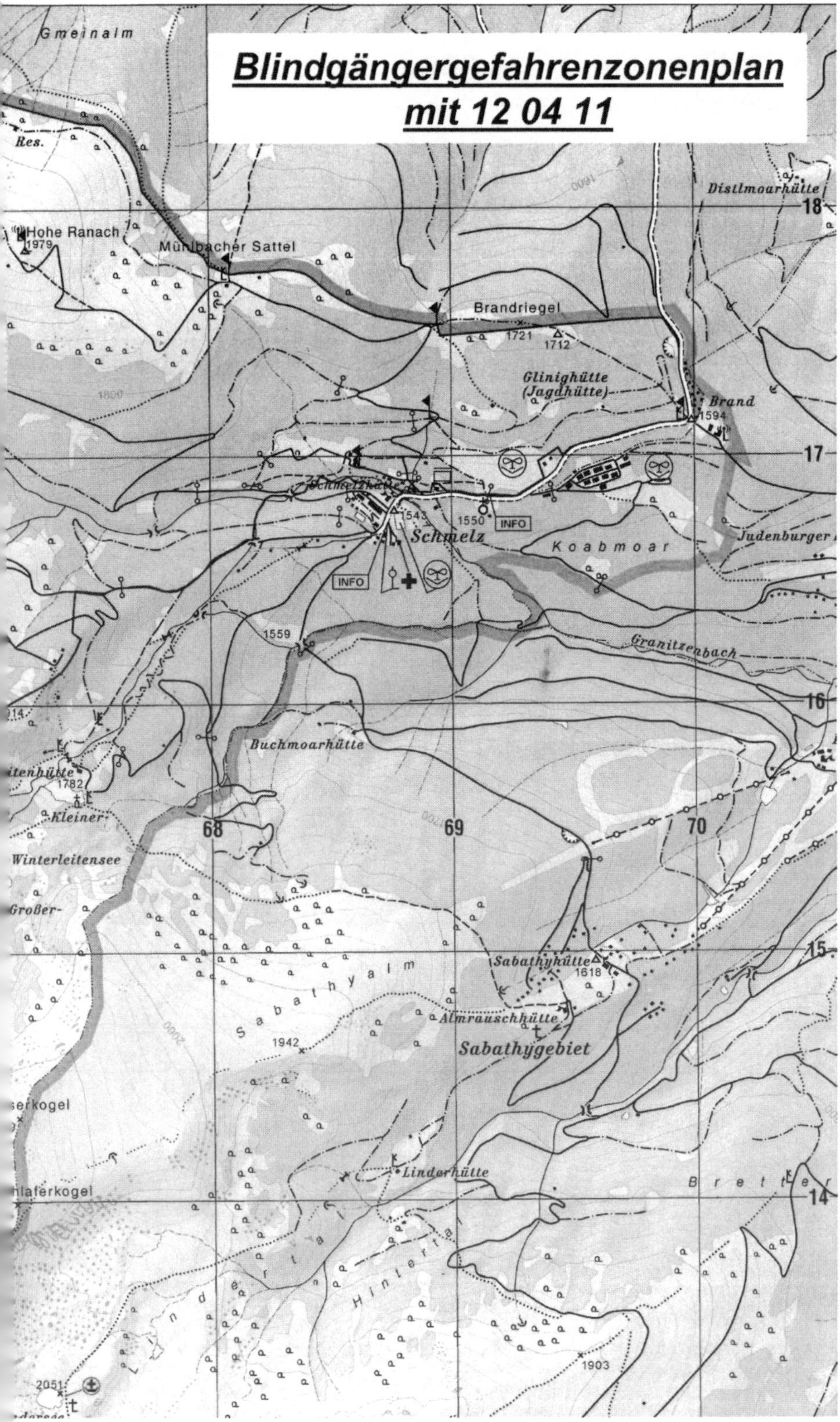

The Seetaler Alps in winter offered a backdrop such as this snow-covered pine forest.

A lake and open pine woodland characteristic of the Seetaler Alps region.

Obdach, the centre point of the pinelands of Steiermark. In the foreground is its parish church.

mental equipment of a sniper', Peter Brookesmith writes, 'involves three vital components: the demoralising effect on the enemy side, the raising of the fighting spirit of his own comrades and the result on the mental and psychological disposition of the would-be or already successful sniper.'[1] Such a sniper constantly has to keep a cool head no matter what might be happening around him. This special quality is that of the experienced hunter. For their opponents, snipers remain invisible. They fire on the chosen enemy with great accuracy of aim from concealment. They lie in wait in the darkness and shoot to a nicety at every glowing point. The sniper is in a position to hold back a far superior enemy force. He may do this by stopping the advance of a company or killing a high-ranking enemy commander with a single round. Mostly

1. Brookesmith, Peter, *Scharfschützen. Geschichte–Taktik–Waffen*, Stuttgart, 2004.

The Obdach town gate.

The Obdach war memorial.

the sniper in his company unit would be told 'Fire at will.' Great successes were obtained by the enemy in his attacks by shooting officers and NCOs. Soviet snipers fired at German soldiers who appeared to have thin legs because they believed that these men were wearing officers' uniforms.

The sniper as an adjunct to the infantry began operations on a scale not previously thought possible during the First World War. With the beginning of trench warfare on the Western Front the hour struck for

> . . . the birth of the sharpshooter's art of the new era. Since the outbreak of war the German Army had begun the introduction of precise hunting rifles with the 7.9 mm army calibre and fitted selected service rifles with telescopic sights. Marksmen with the hunting instinct reaped a harvest of blood amongst the British and French trenches until they too hit upon this new, old fighting art.[1]

1. *Deutsche Militärzeitschrift*, Nr. 77, p. 26.

Sniper training in the World War I Austro-Hungarian Army used 7 mm M-14 repeater rifles with telescopic sight.

The modern entry sign that greets new arrivals at the Seetaler Alps troop-training depot.

Judenburg stands at the north-eastern entrance to the Seetaler Alps troop-training depot.

Snipers achieved true triumphs during the First World War on the fronts in the Dolomites and Carpathian mountains, in the Julian Alps of Slovenia and the Carinthian Alps of Austria and in the twelve battles of the Isonzo.[1]

On patrols the mountain soldier was still the archaic hunter in the truest sense of the word, for he lay in wait for the enemy as if he were wild game, then followed and finished him. It was a fight man against man, an eye for an eye, a tooth for a tooth. Whoever came to grief in this bitter and inescapable struggle to survive might well fall from a steep wall of rock so that his corpse was not infrequently

> . . . horrifically injured, the chest . . . crushed, the bones broken . . . the mouth distorted in the flayed face. The eyes projected in horror from their sockets at the immediate approaching death . . . The heavy rucksack

1. Kaltenegger, Roland, *Deutsche Gebirgstruppen im Ersten Weltkrieg: Von den Dolomiten nach Verdun, von den Karpathen nach Isonzo*, Würzburg, 2014.

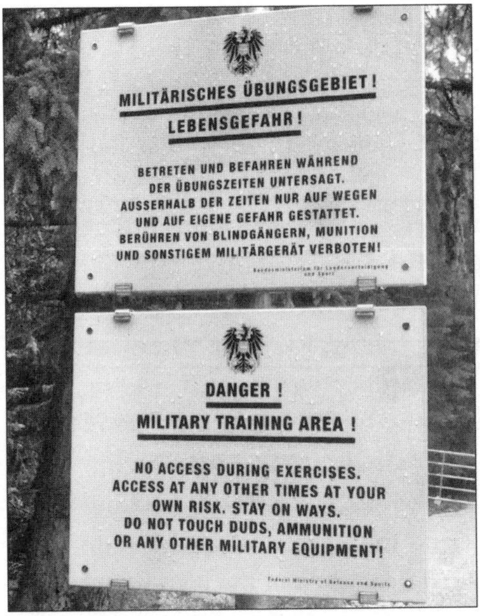

Bilingual warning signs at the troop-training depot.

Target at the rifle range.

Signboard at the Seetaler Alps troop-training depot.

> with its soldiers' comforts still hung from the back of the mute figure.[1]

The decomposing bodies' flesh would soon begin to emit a foul smell . . .

On the Dolomite Front the snipers of the German Alpine Corps as well as those of the Austro-Hungarian infantry inflicted grievous losses on the Italians; just as for their part Italian marksmen made life difficult for their enemy. Even on otherwise quiet days in mountain warfare the sniper was feared. In the war fought in these high mountains the Italians had a dread of Tyrolean sharpshooters and the German High Command even fetched many notorious poachers to what had become a static front. Taking position before first shooting light in a raised hide or in camouflaged brushwood often well forward of his own lines, or from a shell crater or trench, the sniper would follow the movements of the enemy through the telescopic sight. Woe be to the careless individual who showed the least little thing to give himself away. The head shot was always fatal.

Such a sniper needed nerves like wire cable. Of all the branches of service and means of killing used in warfare, no soldier sees the effect of his action so immediately as the sniper, whose bullet ends a man's life abruptly. He is pitted against his victim personally and therefore pulls the trigger in cold blood. The fine line between duty and humanity often comes as a heavy burden for the sniper. In the Second World War the sniper only came into his own when the Eastern Front came to a standstill.

The Soviets also employed female snipers, called by the Germans *Flintenweiber*, 'gun-women'. Lyudmila Pavlichenko from the Ukraine was decorated at Sevastopol for her successes. The undisputed star of the Soviet snipers was a young NCO, Vassili Zaitsev, a shepherd from the Urals said to have killed forty German soldiers in one ten-day period. At Stalingrad he increased his number of kills to 242. His female competitor and lover was the then eighteen-year-old blonde Tanya Chernova. Like him she

1. Schmidkunz, Walter, *Der Kampf über den Gletschern*, 3rd edn., Munich, 1918, p. 214.

Command building of the Seetaler Alps troop-training depot.

shot without emotion and hit 'like a precision machine'. Zaitsev, temporarily blinded by an exploding mine, survived the Second World War as a Hero of the Soviet Union. His lover Chernova, 'who survived a stomach wound usually fatal, lost sight of him after Stalingrad. Not until 1969 did she discover that her teacher and lover was still alive and had married somebody else. According to foreign historians, this was a blow from which she never recovered.'[1]

During the Second World War, the sniper was hailed as a hero not only in the Soviet Union but also in Finland while on the other side 'he was denied recognition by the majority – both military and public'. Then, according to the third most successful Wehrmacht sniper, Lithuanian-born Bruno Sutkus, 'after the war opinion about snipers changed. What he did at the Front was thought of as a crime. His failing was that in duels with enemy snipers he survived, and must live today in the shadows . . .'[2]

1. Zentner, Christian, *Soldaten im Einsatz, Die Deutsche Wehrmacht im Zweiten Weltkrieg*, Hamburg, p. 176.
2. Brookesmith, *Scharfschützen*, p. 72.

This sketch shows a target-judge (Zieler) at the firing range lowering a target to inspect a shooter's accuracy.

Target-judges were often dressed as harlequins. They would mock a rifleman for a poor shot or would make leaps of joy for a good result.

The same applies especially in today's Germany where ex-soldiers of the Wehrmacht in general are often strongly criticised by self-styled 'Remembrance Workers' and *Vergangenheitsbewältiger* ('Those who have come to terms with the past') in their tailor-made penitential robes.

> For the average soldier this may appear unreasonably harsh. He has received no thanks for his service, but it is a fact that most people feel a certain unease about personalities who did their duty very well . . . This discomfort is made worse when the personality exercised an activity bordering on premeditated murder. If we look at our attitude openly and honestly, our relationship towards heroes is of a conflicting nature . . . Heroes

> became heroes because they are necessarily outsiders. The activity of a sniper or marksman implies that he should live his life as an outsider in the armed forces or the police.[1]

Not every hunter succeeded in making a smooth transition from game-hunter to deliberately shooting human beings dead as enemies in wartime.

'During sniper training,' Clifford Shore explained,

> it frequently happened that men would have outstanding results at the shooting stand but fail in the role of sniper. The difference between shooting using a comfortable stance on the shooting range and shooting in wartime, even if one is in a relatively safe spot, could not be greater. Even in a hunt there is a distinct difference, and I have known good marksmen on the firing range who simply could not handle the inner tension of the hunt.[2]

In order to be successful, the sniper must build up an inner defensive wall or armour against which his emotions rebound as though against a metre-thick steel-reinforced concrete wall.

Captain Stephen L. Walsh, active for a period as a sniper-instructor with the US Marine Corps, confirmed: 'We are in a position to see people die, how the head explodes or whatever. That is the thing which does not affect the Pro when he carries out his assignment.'[3]

German sniper training made much use of the Zf. 4-power telescopic sight rifle. Two men who made a good team together would be selected as snipers. They had to have good powers of observation, ability to recognise a target, the ability to describe it precisely, and obviously outstanding accuracy in shooting. A firm hand, nerves like steel and a never-flagging endurance were also required. As well as practical training there was theoretical instruction, including in ballistics and topography.

1. Brookesmith, *Scharfschützen*, p. 73.
2. *Ibid.*, p. 77.
3. *Ibid.*, p. 77.

A soldier who had fought the Soviets in the far north of Russia told Matthäus Hetzenauer during sniper training at Seetaler Alps:

> In the Carelian primaeval forest, the Soviets used snipers who caused us many painful losses. At first we were unprepared for it and therefore had to improvise. We had with us a game warden from Carinthia who in his home mountains was not only a master in protecting wildlife but also one of the best local shots. When he volunteered for the *Gebirgsjäger* he remembered to take with him his telescopic sight, and until the Carelian campaign had carried it around in his rucksack. But now his hour had struck. An armourer mounted it on his carbine and our marksman was ready. When anybody on the enemy side crossed the line of fire of his position, now he fired at once.
>
> But that was still not enough, for Soviet snipers were inflicting grievous losses on our lines and their troops

The remains of an old shooting-stand.

> outnumbered us. He had to have help. But where would one find a source of telescopic sights here, at the top of the world?
>
> Anyway, they gave it a try, called up division and the miracle happened! From which black market they were obtained nobody could tell – but they came, and enough for whole unit. The Carinthian game warden was promoted to corporal and took over the training of the sniper group formed purely of volunteers. The Soviets soon discovered from their personal experience who were the true lords of the sniper war in the Carelian forests. It was a harsh and nerve-racking war and only tailed off when night fell. For the Northern Lights with their luminous beams, which hung from the heavens like a bright veil, were insufficient to guarantee accuracy.

The warning shout, 'Look out, snipers!' sowed panic and fear amongst friend and foe from then on. The marksman with the telescopic sight was now recognised as the ice-cold hunter of men.

As Ernest Hemingway put it: 'Nothing is comparable to hunting human prey, and whoever has hunted people long enough and taken pleasure in it will never give it up.'

A very human situation must not be overlooked:

> A major problem for soldiers on active duty living rough in a confined space such as trenches was the disposal of solid excrement. It was frequently impossible to dig any form of latrine trench, and so the practice of infantrymen was to have a large tin for personal use, which would then be emptied over the trench parapet. This action tended to expose some part of the body and an enemy sniper would have no compunction in accepting the opportunity to fire a bullet into it.[1]

---

1. Wacker, Albrecht: *Sniper on the Eastern Front*, Barnsley, 2005, p. 11. (Translated from the original German publication *Im Auge des Jägers*.)

Chapter 3

Sniper Training and Shooting Techniques

SINCE MATTHÄUS HETZENAUER lacked any front-line experience up to this point, he was now trained at the Seetaler Alps troop-training depot in the shooting techniques of the sniper. From 1944 great value was placed on operational shooting training being as near to the real thing as possible. In his foreword to Army Service Regulations Manual HDV 298/20, 'Battle training for the Soldier Acting Alone', [1] Inspector-General Heinz Guderian wrote:

> The result of the former short-term shooting training was the target-marksman. There was a gaping difference between the first shot from the firing stage and the first live round fired under battle conditions. Because he had not learned to shoot under battle conditions, in battle the rifleman hit nothing.
>
> In shooting, only practical training in the field makes perfect. Therefore in shooting training only those things should be spoken of which play a practical role. In the upshot, the poacher hits his target in the mountains without a clear understanding of the theoretical concepts of shooting lore.

Sniper training for a group initially of twenty men lasted some months. After the first month, those soldiers who did not meet required standards were rejected. Men who wore spectacles were rejected at the outset because glasses misting over, reflecting the

1. *Heeresdienstvorschrift Gefechtsausbildung für den Einzelsoldaten* (HDV 298/20).

Zeichenverkehr beim Schulschießen.

1. Zeichen der schießenden Abteilung.

Feuer.

Halt.

Nochmal anzeigen, oder anzeigen, wenn erst nach mehreren Schüssen angezeigt werden soll.

Rennen durchgeschossen. Bei Übungen, bei denen eine zweite Liste in der Anzeigerdeckung geführt wird, Zeichen dafür, daß die vorher verabredete Anzahl von Schüssen gefallen ist.

Mehrfaches Hochstoßen. Scheibe soll erscheinen.

Schuß gefallen. Anzeigen.

2. Zeichen aus der Anzeigerdeckung.

a) Notzeichen zum Einstellen des Schießens.

Zunächst wird die Scheibe, wenn dies ausführbar ist, in die Deckung gezogen und dann die Tafel wiederholt herausgeschoben  und so lange gezeigt, bis der Leitende oder ein von ihm entsandter Soldat in der Deckung eintrifft.

b) Zeichen zur Benachrichtigung der schießenden Abteilung, daß ihr Zeichen verstanden ist:

Vorschieben der Tafel **1**

95. Sonstige notwendige Sicherheitsmaßnahmen befehlen die Fliegerhorstkommandanten, die für jeden Stand die besonderen Schutzmaßregeln ermitteln (Aufstellen von Posten, Sperren von Durchgängen usw.). Erforderliche Maßregeln werden auf einer Warnungstafel am Eingang des Standes deutlich sichtbar bekanntgegeben.

Message passing by means of semaphore-type signals, as used in Wehrmacht shooting training.

sun or falling off in action caused problems. On the extended shooting field in the Seetaler Alps there were a number of well-disguised targets at up to 800 metres (880 yards) range; principally targets which could be towed or be carried on a pole by men in a

Shooting position 'aiming freehand lying down'.

Shooting position 'aiming sitting at table'.

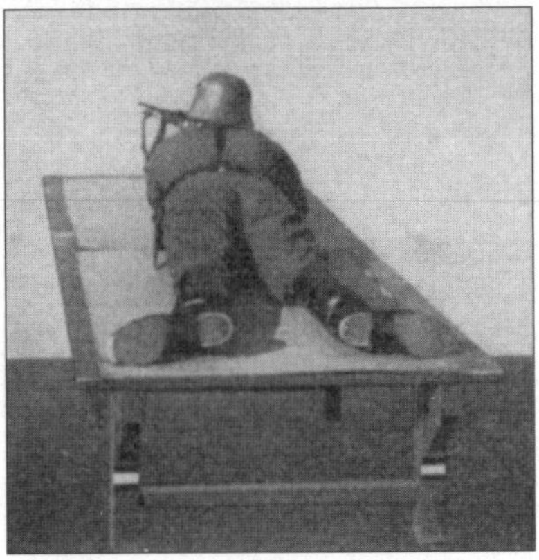

'Aiming freehand lying down.'

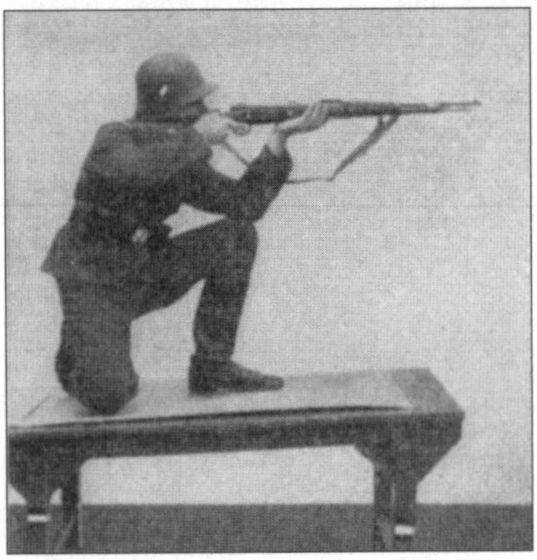

'Aiming kneeling.'

'Aiming kneeling free hand'.

'Aiming standing free hand'.

'Aiming by a tree using cover'.

'Aiming by a tree cradling'.

trench. This manner of representing the target is the nearest to reality for the sniper.

Siegfried F. Hubner wrote:

> After the short basic training there was only one hour's theory per day, and afterwards the trainees could 'fire at will' at targets of all kinds operated by the permanent staff who evaluated their hits. The terrain was well overgrown and a strong wind dominated. It was therefore difficult to hit a moving target when the wind was blowing. The wind was outstandingly suitable for training . . .
>
> Therefore the sniper-trainee reconnoitred the field and watched where the enemy targets briefly made an appearance or moved. Then he did the most important thing, he looked for an optimum position, camouflaged-up and placed himself so that he had a good field of fire but could not be seen. Thus he built a camouflaged sniper's lair with a good support for his rifle. A sniper always fired the SS rifle. The steel helmet would only have got in the way and made it more difficult to hit what was aimed at, therefore it was never worn (unless a superior wanted to play the fool). The important thing was that after a good, well-aimed hit, the sniper was able to retire unnoticed. Snipers always aimed at the head of the enemy – this was what they were taught at the Seetaler Alp – since, after all, in battle the head was often the only part of the body of an enemy, lying in cover, which might be seen momentarily when he fired or was observing. In a trench or when creeping forward in the terrain one would only see the head of an enemy for a brief moment. A sniper was expected to hit a head without fail from 300 to 400 metres range.[1]

The introduction to the 15 May 1943 handbook for the training and deployment of snipers includes the following points:

---

1. Hübner, Siegfried F., *Scharfschützen-Schiesstechnik*, Lichtenwald, 1989, p. 42.

A. Purpose and Task of the Sniper

The purpose of sniper training is to instruct and advance the lone rifleman to the highest performance level of shooting with the rifle. The task of the sniper is to discover small targets difficult of recognition and hit them with a well-aimed single round.

B. Training of the Sniper

1. The Sniper

Only the best marksmen are to be accepted for sniper training. The sniper carries his own rifle with telescopic sight without regard to his rank. A high degree of the hunter's method, patience, endurance and cunning are demanded of the sniper. He must also excel in cold-blooded planning, skilful use of terrain and all possibilities of camouflage, combined with outstanding faculty of observation: as much when creeping up on an enemy position as also in the attack on the enemy.

Determination to get the enemy into his sights whatever the circumstances, to hit and kill him must be specially pronounced in the sniper. It is a distinction to be a sniper.

2, The Instructor

The pre-condition for good shooting training is the selection of a good shooting instructor. He must have experience and an aptitude for teaching, and must also be a first-class marksman. The outstanding qualities of the shooting instructor are calm, patient handling of the idiosyncracies of each rifleman and untiring activity. It is wrong for sniper shooting instruction to be undertaken by group leaders etc., who are unsuitable for the purpose. All company and other unit leaders and shooting instructors must endeavour to encourage the ambitions of the sniper and awaken in him joy in his marksmanship.

Camouflage mask for the face worn here by a Waffen-SS machine-gunner.

Pages 60–75: *Numerous illustrations of snipers' camouflage and means of deceiving the enemy appear in the Introduction of a 15 May 1943 manual for the training and deployment of snipers. They are reproduced here with their original annotations translated.*

A 'birch-tree man'.

Imitation of a tree stump.

Imitation of a pile of stones made out of paper.

Matthäus Hetzenauer wearing his decorations in a photograph probably taken just after the Knight's Cross award ceremony on 17 April 1945. They are: Knight's Cross of the Iron Cross (worn at the neck), German Cross in Gold (lower right pocket of tunic), Iron Cross First Class (left pocket) and Iron Cross Second Class (ribbon in buttonhole), Close Combat Bar in Gold (above left pocket), Sniper Badge in Gold (only top edge of substitute seen here on lower right sleeve), Infantry Attack Badge in Silver and Wound Badge (below Iron Cross, left pocket).

Simon and Magdalena, parents of Matthäus Hetzenauer, as farmers at the Sonnenleithof.

Josef Hetzenauer, the sniper's brother, photographed during his compulsory period with the Reich Labour Service (RAD).

Simon Hetzenauer, the sniper's second brother, who died at the age of eighteen.

The Kufstein barracks where Matthäus Hetzenauer completed his training as a Gebirgsjäger.

Kufstein was the garrison town of 2nd Battalion, 140th Mountain Rifle Regiment.

Gebirgsjäger *marching in close formation through Kufstein.*

Generalleutnant Paul Klatt as the last commander of 3rd Mountain Division.

A Gebirgsjäger *of 3rd Mountain Division after a six-week tour of duty in the southern sector of the Eastern Front.*

Gebirgsjäger *of 144th Mountain Rifle Regiment, 3rd Mountain Division, during a pause in the fighting in the summer of 1944.*

Hetzenauer's regimental comrade-in-arms, sniper Josef Allerberger, who was from the Salzburg area.

Sniper Matthäus Hetzenauer as a member of 144th Mountain Rifle Regiment, 3rd Mountain Division.

3. Gebirgsdivision

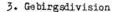

(Vorschlagende Dienststelle)

11. APR. 1945

Vorschlag Nr., 41

für die Verleihung des

Ritterkreuzes zum Eisernen Kreuz

Div.Gef.St., den 10. März 1945

(Klatt)

(Unterschrift, Name in Maschinenschrift)

Generalleutnant und Divisionskommandeur

(Dienstgrad und Dienststellung)

- 3 APR. 1945

Nr.:

An

OKH./PA. 1. Staffel P 5

a. d. D.

The first page of the recommendation for the award of the Knight's Cross to Matthäus Hetzenauer, drawn up on 10 March 1945.

Name	Rufname	Geburtstag und Geburtsort	Dienstgrad, Dienststellung, Dienstverhältnis	Truppenteil	Heimatanschrift (Angabe, ob Ehefrau, Eltern usw.)
Hetzenauer	Matthäus	23.12.24 Brixen im Tale Tirol	Gefreiter Scharfschütze aktive Dienstzeit	7./Geb. Jäg. Rgt. 144	Vater: Simon Hetzenauer Lauterbach im Tale Nr. 156, Kreis Kitzbühel Tirol.

RDA.: —— Diensteintritt: 27.3.1943

Seit wann in letzter Dienststellung: 17. 7.1944

Zugehörigkeit zur Partei bzw. deren Gliederungen mit Dienstrang und -stellung: ——

Beruf des Vorgeschlagenen: (wenn nicht aktiv) Landw. Arbeiter

Friedenstruppenteil des Vorgeschlagenen: (nur bei aktiven Soldaten) ——

Zuständiges Wehrbezirkskommando: (bei Soldaten d. R.) Innsbruck

Beruf des Vaters: Landwirt

Letzte Verwundung am 6.11.44 A.G. Kopf (bei der Truppe verblieben)

Ist mit der Wiederherstellung der Frontverwendungsfähigkeit zu rechnen? ——

Bisher verliehene Kriegsauszeichnungen mit Angabe der Verleihungsdaten		Bisherige Kriegsverwendung seit 1939 mit Angabe der Daten	
E.K. 2.Klasse	am 1. 9. 1944	27. 3.43 – 1. 7.43	Grundausbildung m.Gr.W.-Schütze
E.K. 1.Klasse	am 25.11. 1944	2. 7.43 – 26. 3.44	uk.- gestellt
Verw.Abz.Schwarz	am 9.11. 1944	27. 3.44 – 16. 7.44	Ausbildung als Scharfschütze
Inf.Sturmabzeichen Silber	am 13.11. 1944	17. 7.44 – jetzt	Scharfschütze
Scharfschützenabzeichen in Gold	am 3.12. 1944		
	am 19		
	am 19		
	am 19		
	am 19		
	am 19		

Hetzenauer's personal details and his decorations to that point are listed in the recommendation for the award of the Knight's Cross (above). The report by Generalleutnant Paul Klatt advocating the award and endorsed by General von Le Suire is above right. By 10 March 1945 Hetzenauer had 172 confirmed kills, so that in the following sixty days to the capitulation he was successful on a further 174 occasions.

Kurze Begründung und Stellungnahme der Zwischenvorgesetzten:

Gefreiter Hetzenauer hat sich als Scharfschütze durch besonders hervorragende Einsatzfreude und tollkühnes Kämpfertum ausgezeichnet. In der Zeit vom 1.9.44 - 10.3.1945 hat er 172 bestätigte Scharfschützenabschüsse erzielt. H., ein einfacher, bescheidener Jäger, kämpft täglich ohne Befehl im selbständigen Handeln mit einer beispiellosen Tapferkeit unermüdlich und ohne Rücksicht auf dauernd drohende Lebensgefahr und wurde durch seine tollkühnen Unternehmungen als Einzelkämpfer divisionsbekannt. Die meisten seiner Abschüsse erzielte H. dadurch, daß er sich vorwärts der eigenen H.K.L. unmittelbar vor den feindlichen Stellungen einnistet und dort ohne Rücksicht auf eigenes oder feindliches Artilleriefeuer oder feindliche Angriffe oder Stoßtruppunternehmungen sich seine Opfer sucht.

So hatte er am 2.2.45 allein während eines feindlichen Angriffsunternehmens, wieder vor den feindlichen Stellungen liegend, 18 Scharfschützenabschüsse erzielt. H. hat damit allein als Gesamtergebnis zwei kampfkräftige feindliche Kompanien außer Gefecht gesetzt und im eigenen Handeln somit einen Erfolg über den Rahmen seines eigenen Wirkungsbereiches hinaus erzielt.

Klatt

(Klatt)
Generalleutnant u. Divisionskommandeur

Generalkommando XXXXIX. (Geb.) A.K.
- Abt. II a Az. 29 / RK

K.Gef.Std., den 16.3.1945

U.

Armeegruppe Heinrici -IIa-.

Der Vorschlag der 3.Geb.Division zur Verleihung des Ritterkreuzes des Eisernen Kreuzes an den Scharfschützen Gefr. Hetzenauer, 7./Geb.Jäg.Rgt.144, wird befürwortet.

v. Le Suire

(v. Le Suire)
General der Gebirgstruppe
u.Kommandierender General.

1. Panzer-Armee	
Eing. 19 III 1945	
Nr.:	
Anl.: 2x	
Bearb.Abt. IIa RK	

Matthäus Hetzenauer of 7th Company, 144th Mountain Rifle Regiment, 3rd Mountain Division. Seen here in the uniform of a Gefreiter *as indicated by the single chevron on the upper sleeve, he was the most successful sniper of the German Wehrmacht.*

The award of the Knight's Cross to Matthäus Hetzenauer on 17 April 1945 at Friedberg (Mährisch-Ostrau). Note the Close Combat Bar above the left pocket of his tunic.

Sniper Oberjäger Jakob Hechl of 91st Mountain Rifle Regiment, 4th Mountain Division.

At the end of the war most of the survivors could expect captivity.

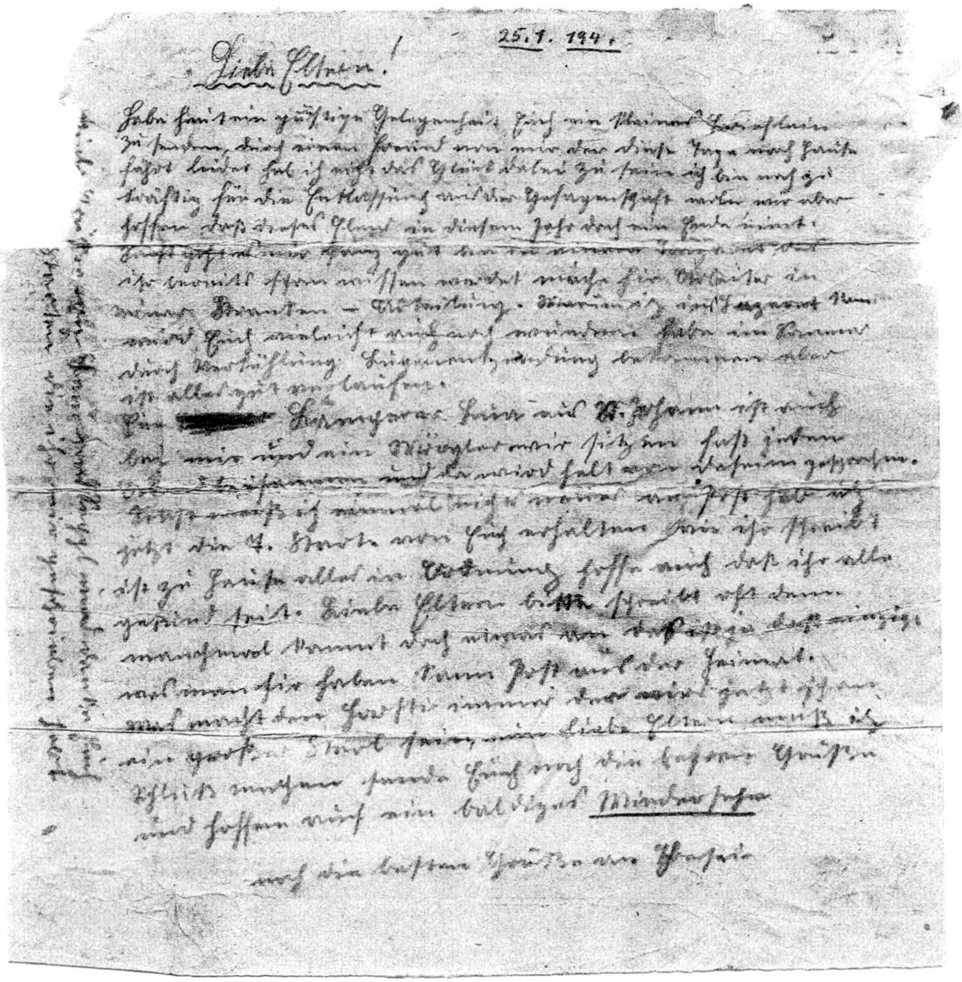
25.1.194.

Liebe Eltern!

The inside of the tobacco pouch used by Matthäus Hetzenauer with a message in tiny script in order to include as many words as possible for his parents.

Visit of the pretender to the Austrian throne, Otto von Habsburg (centre with tie), to the Sonnleithof. At his left shoulder are parents Simon and Magdalena, at his right shoulder Matthäus Hetzenauer; the boy at the end is Hetzenauer's son Hermann.

Otto von Habsburg greeting Magdalena Hetzenauer. Behind her with the hat is her husband Simon.

Group photo of the Comradeship reunion on 15 May 1999 at Itter in the Brixental. Matthäus Hetzenauer is in the centre of the photograph, fifth from the left in the second row.

The author Roland Kaltenegger inspecting documents in the Hetzenauer family's hunting room.

20 | BILD am SONNTAG, 1. März 2015

Seit Donnerstag im Kino: Der umstrittene US-Film „American Sniper“ mit Bradley Cooper als Scharfschütze Chris Kyle. Regie: Clint Eastwood

Der Wehrmachtsgefreite Matthäus Hetzenauer bekam das Ritterkreuz, nachdem er 345 alliierte Soldaten tödlich getroffen hatte

1805 fiel der britische Admiral Horatio Nelson in der Seeschlacht von Trafalgar durch den Schuss eines Scharfschützen

Der legendäre Wilhelm Tell gilt als erster Sniper. Er musste seinem Sohn mit der Armbrust einen Apfel vom Kopf schießen

Scharfschützen – der Mythos stirbt zuletzt

An article in the Bild am Sonntag *newspaper of 1 March 2015: ‘Snipers – the Myth dies at last’. The caption beside the photo of Hetzenauer reads: ‘The Wehrmacht private Matthäus Hetzenauer received the Knight’s Cross after killing 345 Allied soldiers.’*

The badges, orders and decorations of Matthäus Hetzenauer.

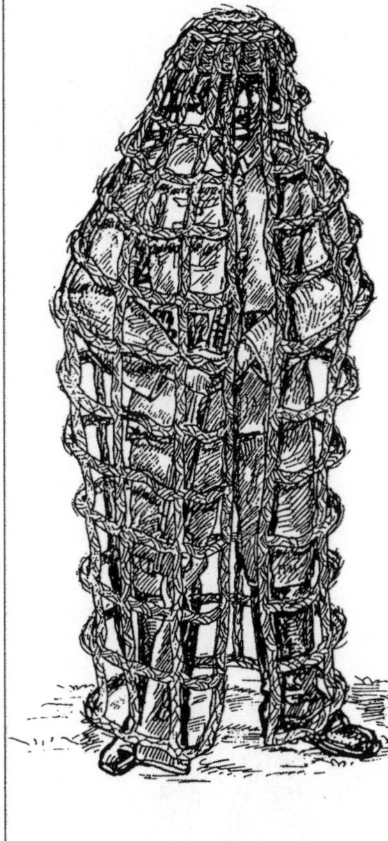

A net-like 'plaited undercoat' for attaching all kinds of camouflage.

A longitudinal 'plaited coat' made out of grass.

A 'Florentine Hut'.

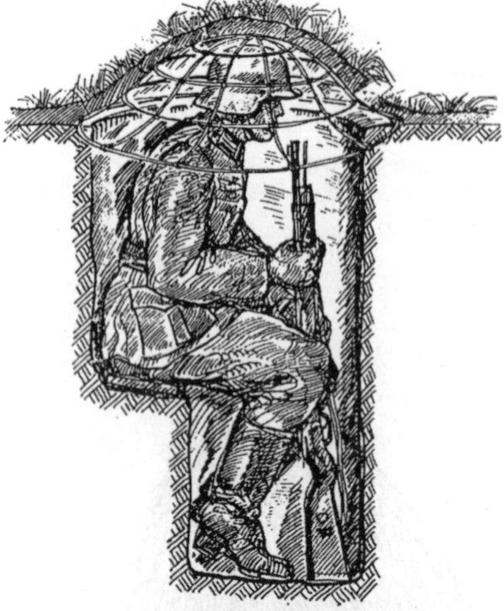

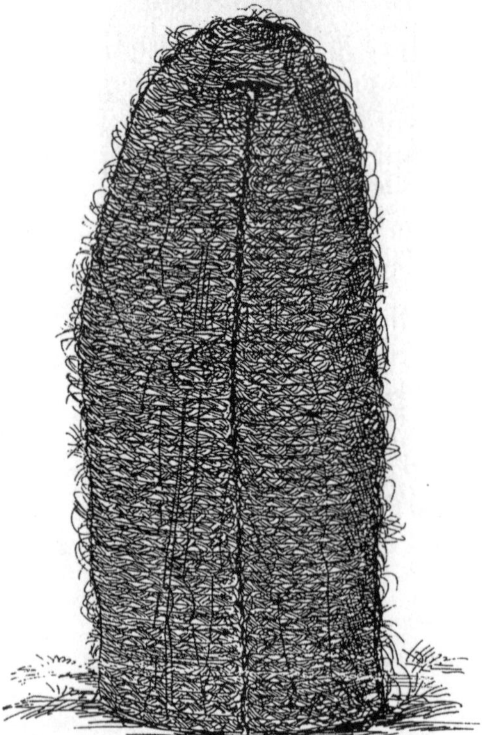

A sniper in a 'beehive'.

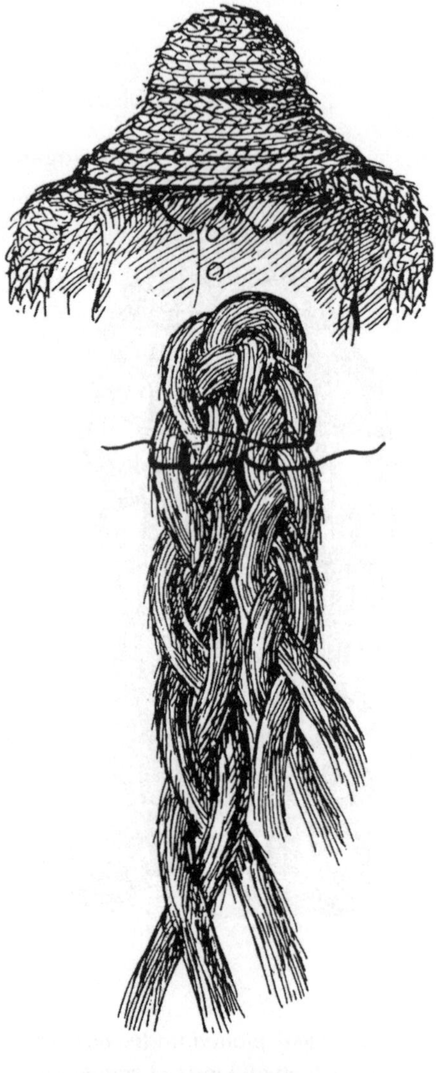

A plaited 'camouflage hat' showing plaitwork below.

3. Instruction

Practical instruction in shooting is to be prepared for by instruction about the weapon, the telescopic sight, shooting instruction and sandbox practice. Instruction must be limited to the essentials in a simple, short and clear manner . . .

7. Estimating Distance

The basis for shooting accuracy is precise estimation of the range. Exercises must be carried out in various kinds of terrain, in all kinds of weather and at all times of day. Distances are to be calculated from all body positions. The sniper must be able to estimate very precisely distances up to 500 metres [550 yards] . . . Distances tend to be underestimated when the target is clearly visible – in sunshine – with the sun at the sniper's back – and especially over water, snow and plains – when it is impossible to see into individual stretches of terrain – with a bright ground or background . . .

10. Camouflage and Deception

Besides technical shooting ability the sniper in the field requires masterly camouflage and to play a waiting game based on deception. Some suggestions for camouflage, stalking and creating an illusion are provided in the following pages. In many cases the illustrations are incomplete. Reference has not been made to the actual use of camouflage suits, parkas and camouflage nets. Camouflage face-nets and long camouflage gloves are the best disguise for face and hands! The suggestions can be further developed and completed using one's own ideas and suggestions. In the periods set aside for make and mend the sniper must learn how to prepare the necessary materials by improvisation.

In 1944 the 'Ten Commandments for German Snipers' were:

1. Fight fanatically!
2. Shoot calmly and deliberately: what matters most is not how fast you can fire but getting a hit.
3. Your most deadly opponent is the enemy sniper! Be smarter than him.
4. Never fire more than once from your position, otherwise they will spot you.
5. The entrenching tool lengthens your life.
6. Constantly practise distance estimation.
7. Be a master of camouflage and in the use of terrain.
8. Maintain your shooting skill through constant practice, even behind the front and when at home.
9. Never let your sniper's rifle out of your hand. The well-maintained weapon is your strength . . .
10. The important rule for survival is camouflage-up ten times, and shoot once.

Absolutely essential qualities of the sniper are always:

1. Assessment of the terrain.
2. The line of retreat.
3. The best possible camouflage.
4. Good nerves and concentration even when under enemy fire.
5. A precisely calibrated telescopic-sight rifle.
6. Correct estimation of distance, temperature and the influence of high ground.
7. Cunning deception of the enemy.
8. Correct manner of dealing with moving targets.

Army Regulation HDV 298/20 for snipers states:

> The sniper must be trained to be a hunter who stalks enemy prey with loose, easy, supple movements, skilfully using all advantages of ground cover and terrain, camouflages himself for invisibility and waits with the calm of the hunter until his prey is 'ready for the shot', which is to say is in the best position to be killed

'Camouflage of fringes' (grasses, grass bundles, pine-leaf bundles).

'Camouflage fans' of wire.

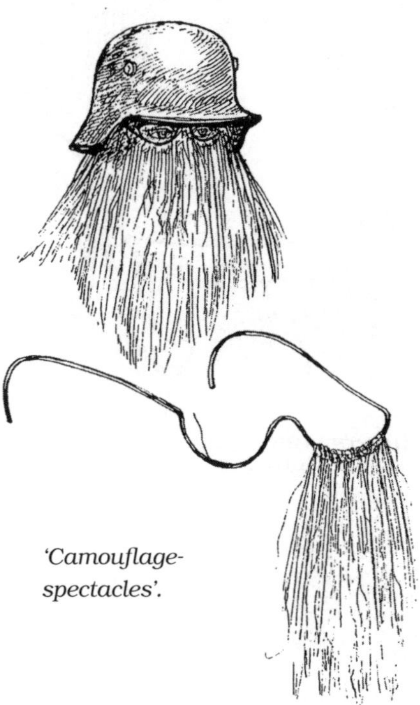

'Camouflage-spectacles'.

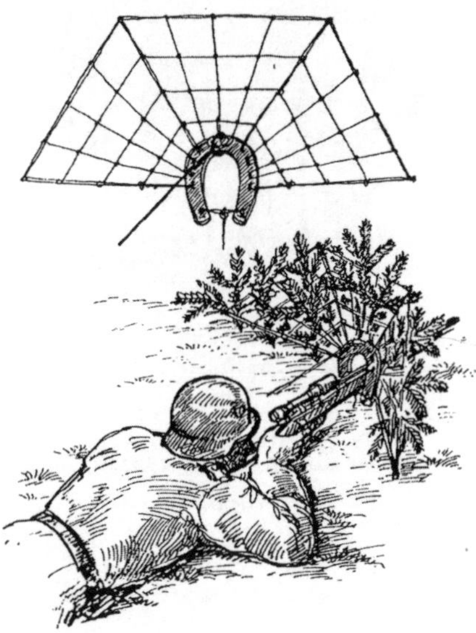

Sniper disguised as a bush, from the front.

Sniper disguised as a bush, from the rear.

Net suit head-to-toe for all disguises.

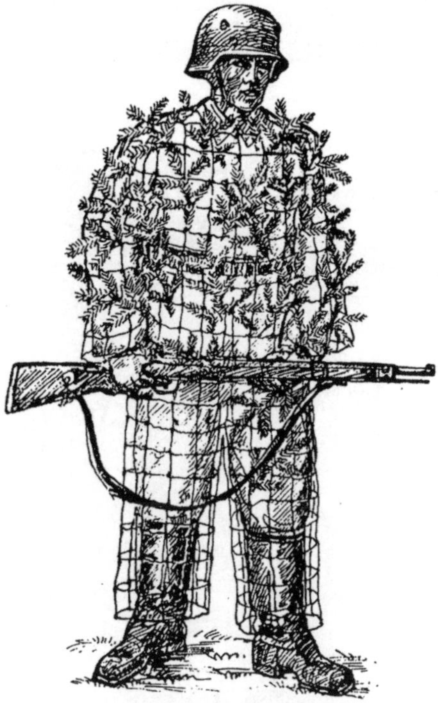

Polish camouflage net suit.

Stalking frame with rifle sledge.

Covered-over trough.

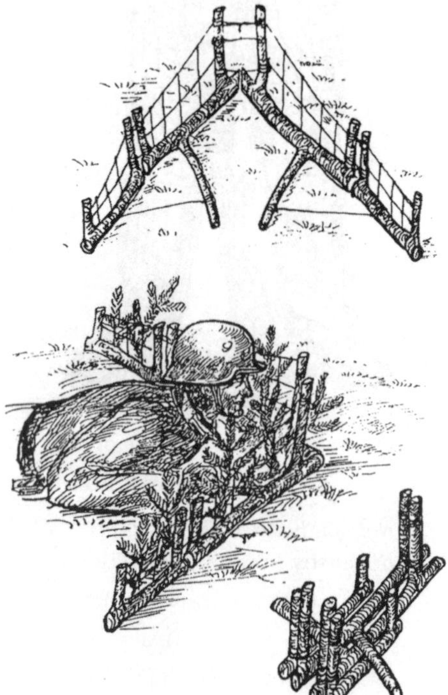

Stalking frame.

Wooden camouflage fan.

with a well-aimed round to the head. The sniper is distinguished by cunning, versatility, camouflage and outstanding shooting technique.

Circular 25b/36 for the deployment and use of snipers makes clear:

1. The sniper is a carefully trained specialist. He is equipped with an especially good sniper's rifle and special ammunition with which he has made himself thoroughly familiar during training and which he has calibrated. As a result he knows the characteristics of his weapon and knows the importance of caring for it. He alone is responsible for the rifle and equipment. He must be given the opportunity to check its calibration and rectify any inexactitude. It is forbidden to relieve him of his rifle and equipment without compelling reason or to train other snipers with it and use it for their shooting training.
2. Besides thorough training in shooting, the special training of the sniper principally covers: a hunter-like, very cunning approach, patience and endurance, masterly use of the land and disguise. The sniper has learnt that what matters for him is not a high rate of fire, but only that with every round fired he obtains a hit.
3. Generally speaking, the sniper does not take part in an assault, but supports his attacking troops by eliminating especially dangerous enemy targets. Engaging the enemy at a range of over 400 metres only pays off against larger targets that can be seen clearly. Snipers should work in pairs if possible or with one sniper supported by an observer. They then assist each other to recognise targets, watch out for stalkers, deceive enemy snipers, observe accuracy of fire, provide protection when withdrawing from the enemy. Snipers can be included within the company or battalion. The sniper should fire from a particular position at the most 3–5 times. Therefore he must prepare beforehand a well-camouflaged new

'Red Indian's cap' of wire (designed to disguise every head movement).

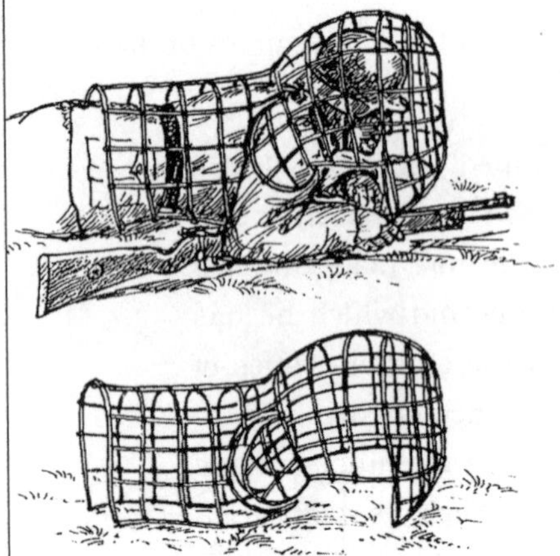

Camouflage net for creeping up.

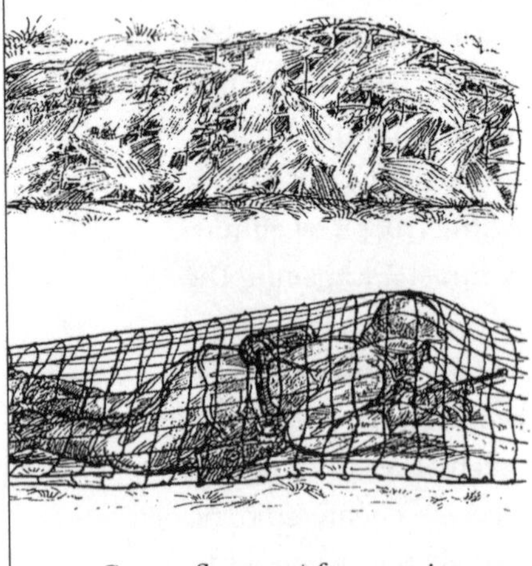

Camouflage net for creeping up.

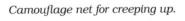

Mannequin attached to a long pole.

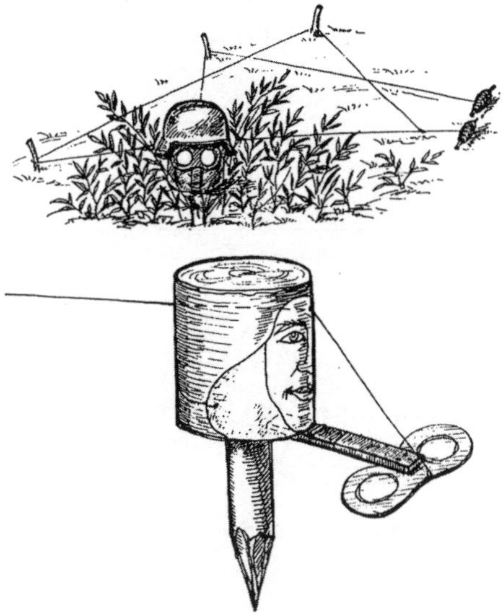

A mannequin-observer.

Head of mannequin which travels along a trench.

Making an artillery scissor-telescope mock-up occasionally visible by parting a bush.

Mannequin 'looking through binoculars'.

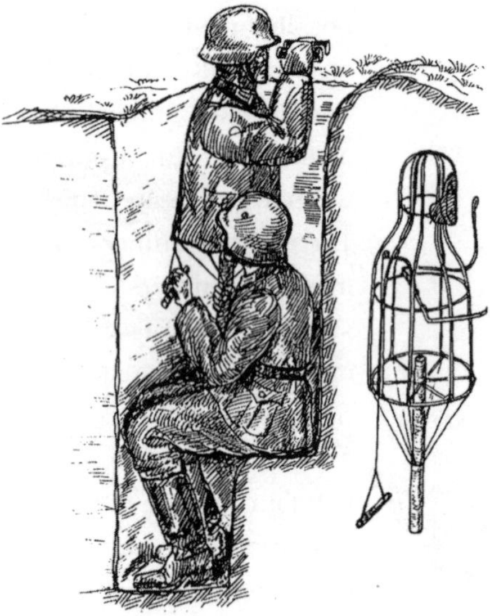

Mannequin 'having a smoke'.

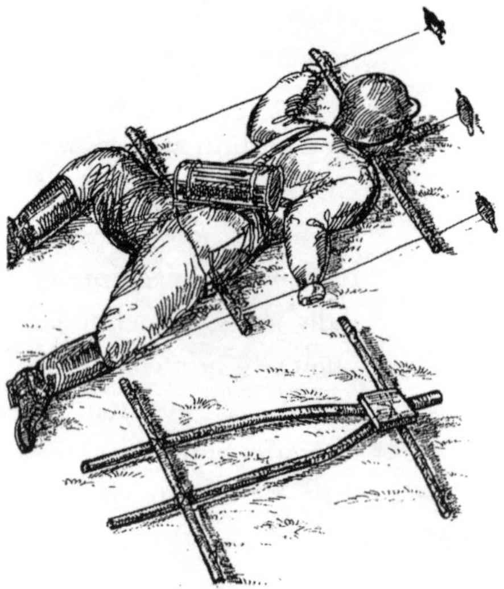

Mannequin 'sneaking forward'.

position that he will be able to reach under cover. If possible positions must allow engagement of the enemy on the flanks and offer frontal cover against being seen and fired at. Snipers should never adopt a position near a machine gun. Coupling sniper fire with indirect-fire weapons (rifle-grenades, mortars) is especially effective. Targets for snipers are: officers, snipers, observers, message-runners, crews of heavy guns, sentries, shooting embrasures. The hours of main activity are daybreak and dusk, and those times when the enemy has his meals and changes of shift.

4. On the defensive, according to the situation, the sniper will join the line of outposts in or behind the main front line and lie in wait. Here, as for a hunter, it may often be hours before a favourable moment presents itself for a shot. No careless movement of the enemy ought to escape his notice. He must know the trench systems and customs of the enemy precisely. It is expedient to prepare a sketch of the enemy line with aiming points in order that results observed may be plotted as quickly as possible and the range gauged swiftly and precisely for a certain shot. When a unit is withdrawing from the enemy the sniper acts as a rearguard.

5. Special achievements by the sniper should be recognised by decorations and rewards (mentions in daily orders, mentions in despatches, special leave, photograph of commanding officer with dedication and signature, gifts from Army stores). An operation with difficult conditions, for example hours or days lying in wait, justifies freedom from duty rosters for the sniper and approval for suitable ration supplements, like canned foods, biscuits, crackers.

During active service on the southern Eastern Front, Hetzenauer was given a multitude of targets to engage and also carried out difficult and dangerous missions of reconnaissance and spying out the terrain. This included strategically important crossroads,

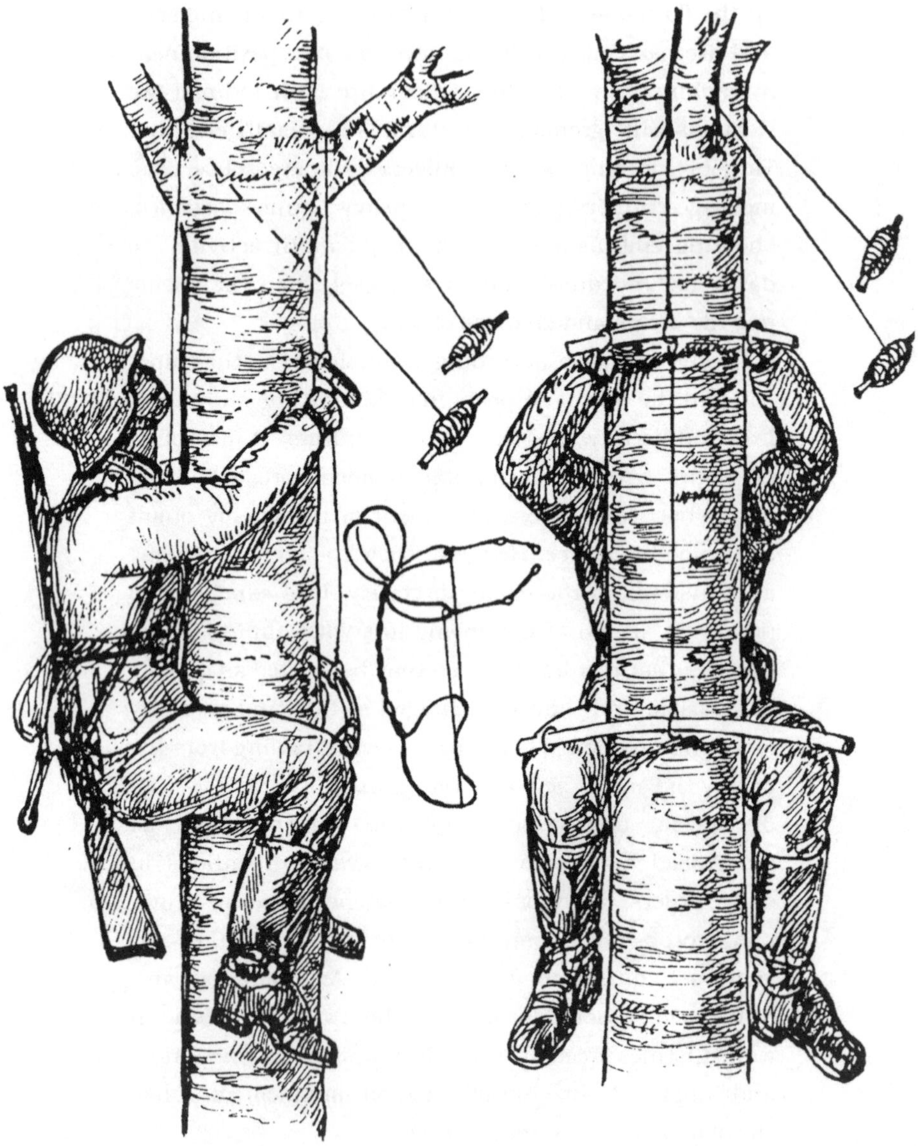

Mannequin 'climbing a tree'.

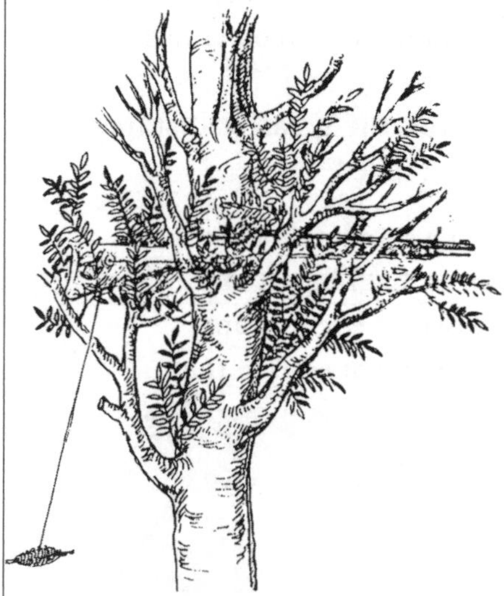

A tree with a self-loading rifle.

Mannequin which rises and shoots.

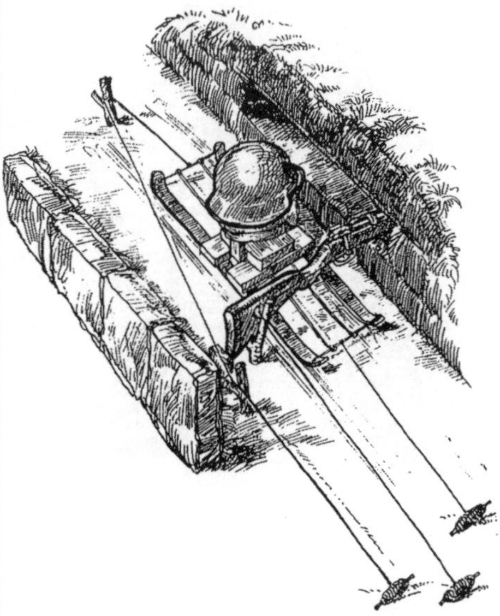

Mannequin's head seen 'firing' from a bunker slit.

Mannequin which goes to ground and shoots.

bridges, airfields, railway lines, telephone installations and other key features, both in the normal terrain and in the Carpathians, for 'snipers are in a position to secure, monitor, seal off or destroy targets of that kind'.[1]

Hetzenauer was once asked what was the greatest distance over which he had fired at an enemy. He replied,

> About 1,100 metres [1,200 yards] at a standing soldier. It was not likely that I would hit him at that range, but the shot was necessary under the existing circumstances in order to make it clear to the enemy that even at that range he should not feel safe.

---

1. Brookesmith, *Scharfschützen*, p. 98.

Chapter 4

The Sniper Badge

BY VIRTUE OF THE EXTREMELY RISKY nature of their duties in the Second World War, and on account of their extraordinary bravery in the pitiless circumstances of the front, during the first years of the war the most successful snipers of the German Wehrmacht were awarded the Iron Cross, First and Second Class. In order to distinguish them particularly from men in other branches of service

Besitzzeugnis

Dem

(Dienstgrad)

(Vor- und Familienname)

(Truppenteil)

wurde das

Scharfschützenabzeichen (Stufe)

verliehen.

(Ort und Datum)

(Dienststempel)

(Unterschrift)

DIN A 6 H

(Dienstgrad und Dienststellung)

9

The achievements of a sniper were given special recognition by the award of the Sniper Badge in one of its grades (overleaf), *and the certificate confirming the award* (above).

Sniper's Badge in Gold.

who had also excelled themselves against the enemy, divisions had awarded special certificates and badges of recognition of their own before the official introduction of a Sniper Badge.

The need to recognise the service rendered by snipers was more clearly seen by commanders at the front than by the national leaders and therefore much time passed before the inauguration of the Sniper Badge. Not until 20 August 1944, therefore, a month after the unsuccessful attempt on Hitler's life, did the *Führer* and

Oil painting of the sniper Matthäus Hetzenauer.

Sniper aiming, using a rifle with telescopic sight.

Supreme Commander of the Wehrmacht issue a *Führerbefehl* introducing the Sniper Badge which was to have equivalent status to the Iron Cross, First Class. The order read:

> 1. In recognition of the important tactical employment of the lone warrior with rifle as sniper, and to honour the successes achieved thereby, I introduce for the Army and Waffen-SS the Sniper Badge. The badge will be awarded in three grades.
> 2. The conditions relevant thereto will be drawn up by the General of Infantry advising the Chief of the Army General Staff.

The relevant conditions from the Army High Command followed in parallel with the publication of the *Führerbefehl*. These stated:

> The Führer has introduced a Sniper Badge for the Army and Waffen-SS. This is to honour the important tactical employment of the lone rifleman and his successes with aimed single shots, and at the same time to act as an incentive to increase the achievements to date. Therefore the Sniper Badge is to be awarded in accordance with the following principles:
> 1. The Sniper Badge will be awarded by the nearest field officer with the competence of at least a regimental commander to such soldiers who have received planned sniper training and are employed as such, and based on the written recommendation of the unit leader. The soldier so awarded is to receive a certificate of the award (Certificate of Possession, Sniper Badge Grade —) and an entry is to be made in his personal record.
> 2. The Badge comes in three grades and is to be worn on the lower right sleeve.
> 3. The grades are as follows:
> Grade 1 for at least twenty hits after 1 September 1944 inclusive (badge without border).
> Grade 2 for at least forty hits after 1 September 1944 inclusive (badge with silver cord trim).

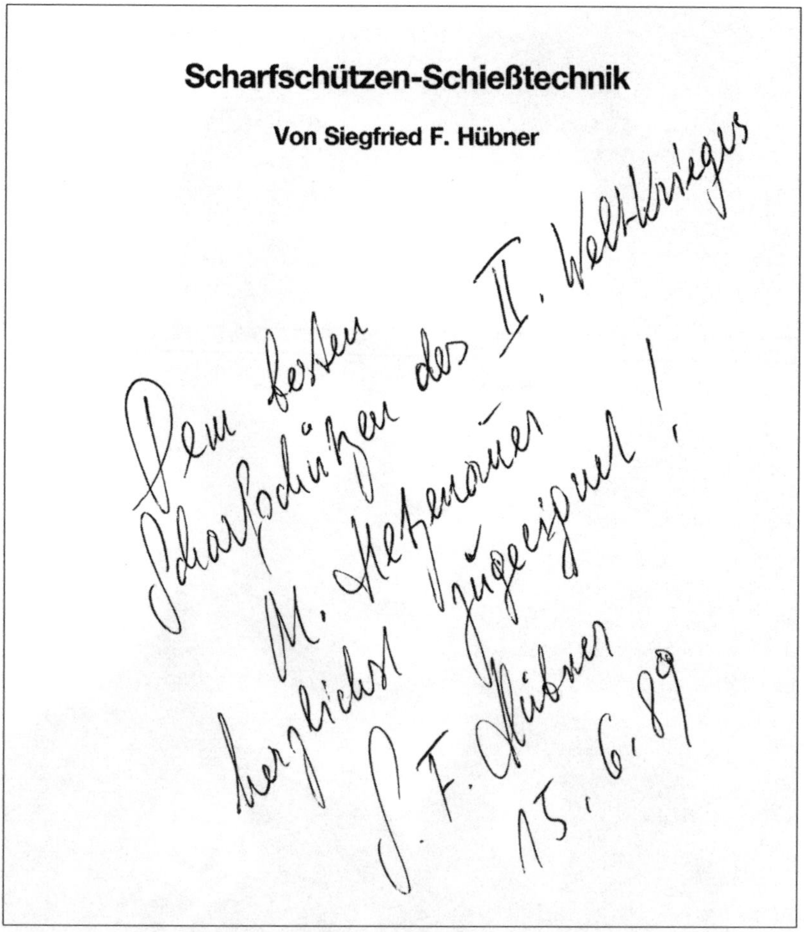

Scharfschützen-Schießtechnik

Von Siegfried F. Hübner

Dem besten Scharfschützen des II. Weltkrieges M. Hetzenauer herzlichst zugeeignet! S. F. Hübner 15.6.89

Many decades after the Second World War Matthäus Hetzenauer received from its author a copy of Siegfried F. Hubner's book Scharfschützen-Schiesstechnik. *The handwritten inscription reads: 'To the best sniper of the Second World War, M. Hetzenauer, a heartfelt dedication!'*

Grade 3 for at least sixty hits after 1 September 1944 inclusive (badge with gold cord trim).

Hits obtained in close combat are not to count, moreover the enemy soldier must have been capable of movement and have not signalled his intention to defect or surrender.

Left: *Gefreiter der reserve Matthäus Hetzenauer, photographed wearing the Iron Cross First Class and Second Class.*

Reichsführer-SS Heinrich Himmler.

4. For every claimed hit a report is to be submitted to the unit together with confirmation by at least one witness (officer or NCO). In order to avoid unnecessary correspondence, there will be no retrospective credit of hits before the effective date. It is suggested that the

previous successes of snipers be spread across all the troops in the form of Iron Crosses.

Oberkommando des Heeres, 20 August 1944.

In order to motivate and encourage men of the Waffen-SS to become snipers, Heinrich Himmler wrote to Armaments Minister Albert Speer on the subject of sniper training on 18 December 1944 suggesting supplementary rewards for snipers. He accepted that 'theoretically on the Eastern Front alone around 20,000 enemy soldiers can be killed by snipers each month if enough sniper rifles and telescopic sights are made available'. Therefore the Reichsführer-SS promised:

1. After 50 confirmed hits the award of a watch.
2. After 100 confirmed hits the sniper will be invited to hunt deer or chamois with the Reichsführer-SS.

Chapter 5

With 3rd Mountain Division, 1944–1945

A PROBLEM CONFRONTS the biographer of a sniper which can be expressed through the saying, 'The winner was in the right and the loser in the wrong.' So, while Soviet and Allied marksmen have been honoured as heroes, German and Austrian snipers have been seen as evil assassins.

Strangely this is the case in their own countries too. Not surprisingly nearly all chose to shut out their experiences as though they never happened. This explains why personal accounts are so rare and sought after.[1]

After his in-depth training as a sniper at the Seetaler Alps troop-training ground in Steiermark, on 17 July 1944 Matthäus Hetzenauer was transferred from 379th March Battalion (Special Purposes) to 7th Company, 144th Mountain Rifle Regiment, 3rd Mountain Division, as a sniper. This important division of mountain troops was in the thick of the fighting on the southern sector of the Eastern Front under a new commander, Generalmajor Paul Klatt.[2] Therefore, a few days short of his twentieth birthday, Hetzenauer had little time to familiarise himself with the routine of a fighting force and its officers and men. Fortunately 'the enemy activity for the near future led us to expect a quiet period of trench warfare', Klatt wrote.

> We were facing two relatively weak enemy groups in the 38th Rifle Division and 159th Fortified Sector. They had

1. Wacker, Albrecht, *Sniper on the Eastern Front*, pp. xiii–xiv.
2. Kaltenegger, Roland, *Generalleutnant Paul Klatt, Vom Gebirgspionier zum letzten Kommandeur der 3. Gebirgsdivision*, Würzburg, 2014, p. 108*ff.*

From left, Oberstleutnant Lorch, a Romanian officer and General Klatt.

Gebirgsjäger *of 3rd Mountain Division during the retreat in Russia, 1944.*

Soviet paratroop landings in the southern sector of the Eastern Front, 1944.

no radio discipline and therefore soon provided us with very useful reports about their tactical organisation and intentions. Battlefield activities on both sides during the following weeks were limited to scouting and small assault parties, occasional artillery exchanges and sporadic fire by our snipers, greatly feared by the Soviets. Trench warfare! At last we had the time to sort ourselves out and freshen up. We were not a spent force. We had kept our small core of officers and NCOs well tried and tested in many actions, and strong battalions of reinforcements were coming up from the Reich . . .

Soon the companies and battalions were back to full strength. A host of new arrivals brought inspiration and comradeship, in the groups from man to man, into the upper levels and from one branch of service to another . . .

Soviet infantry crossing a small river.

> There was no drill but the commanders looked on and ensured that the fighting abilities of their force developed. There were difficulties in obtaining weapons and equipment but these were finally overcome. Oberst Kreppel did not rest until the last missing mountain gun had been replaced.
>
> Looking back, this period on the Moldau gave us a last chance to take a breath before the curtain rose on the bloody final act of this dramatic war.[1]

It was not too long in coming. The Red Army broke through at Brody on the Styr Front, a fact of which Klatt learned on 14 July 1944. It alarmed him, for he knew the suction effect of that kind of major battle on more distant front sectors only too well from his experience of previous withdrawals on the Eastern Front.

The 8th Rifle Division, the northern neighbour of 3rd Mountain Division, pushed north-west to the upper Bug, and the *Gebirgsjäger* received orders to extend their sector by 55 kilometres (34 miles)

1. Klatt, Paul, *Die 3. Gebirgsdivision 1939–1945*, Bad Nauheim, 1958. p. 278*f.*

to the north-west to plug the gap. They now had responsibility for a sector of the Gebirgs-Front over 90 kilometres (55 miles) long. The new defensive strongpoint was the railway line at Gura Humorului. From there the main front line ran for around 50 kilometres (30 miles) through thick woodlands before gaining 600 metres (1,970 feet) in altitude to the 1,200-metre (3,940-f00t) high peaks of the Carpathians.

The failed assassination attempt of 20 July 1944 on the life of the *Führer* surprised the officers and men serving at the front. A short while before NSFO (National Socialist Leadership Officers) had been attached to 3rd Mountain Division where they associated only with the officers and NCOs. Meanwhile divisional instructors were training Romanian units unaware that Romania was about to defect from the Axis.

In the early hours of 19 August the Red Army commenced its campaign on the Carpathian Front by heavy artillery fire against 3rd Mountain Division trenches, and a little later a newly formed Soviet rifle division came up from Solca in four spearheads. The Romanian *Ghergel* Battalion, integrated into the sector of 2nd Battalion, 138th Mountain Rifle Regiment, abandoned the two heights it occupied after a few rounds of Soviet sniper fire.

On 20 August General Klatt was wounded while organising a counter-attack by 112th Field Reinforcement Battalion north of Frumosul. After a difficult ascent his men encountered a far stronger enemy force. His mountain batteries gave what support they could, 'Nevertheless the struggle for Height 1,055 in the thick mountain woodlands became a kaleidoscope of fast-changing battle situations,' he wrote.

> In my mind's eye I still see the bloody duels between our men and enemy riflemen in the trees, throwing our weapons around to defend against an ambush, scouting a thicket, ever in doubt as to whether it concealed friend or foe. By the end of this woodland battle with its high losses, however, our field reinforcement battalion had managed to erect the protective barrier ordered.[1]

1. *Ibid.*, p. 282.

On the morning of 23 August the counter-attack by 138th Mountain Rifle Regiment began. Two attack groups, *Griessler* and *Zeppner*, were made up from its 1st and 3rd Battalions plus 3rd Company, 83rd Mountain Pioneer Battalion, commanded by Oberleutnant Herbert Hintze. Heights 131 and 1209 at the rear of 2nd Battalion were the target. 'The Soviets defended bitterly,' Klatt recalled:

> Height 1103 was stormed by the riflemen and pioneers. Despite the torrential rain they had almost mopped up by midday. Next day Height 1209 also fell to us after riflemen fought their way to within 400 metres of it during the night.[1]

First General Staff Officer Oberst von Eimannsberger summed up this victory in his personal diary thus:

> Wireless observation reported that the Soviet 240th Rifle Division ordered the attack broken off. The situation at 112th Field Reinforcement Battalion is stable. 2nd Battalion, 138th Mountain Rifle Regiment, reports re-munitioning and shipping out of wounded. The rear of this battalion is cleansed!

Shortly afterwards alarming reports were received at 3rd Mountain Division to the horror of Generalmajor Klatt that Romanian troops had abandoned their Axis partner. This meant a very dangerous situation for 3rd Mountain Division. The commanders and NCOs were speaking quite openly of the Romanian treachery, by which they had been struck as if out of a clear blue sky, for the policy change of the Romanian leaders had important consequences for their troops in the 3rd Mountain Division sector.

> On that night of betrayal [General Klatt wrote], we were also overwhelmed by events. Towards 2300 hrs 2nd Battalion, 144th Mountain Rifle Regiment, battalion commander Major Kloss, asked the divisional

1. Klatt, *Die 3. Gebirgsdivision 1939–1945*, p. 282.

A soldier not recognisable at first glance as a German sniper leaving his former hideout in a wrecked Soviet T-34 tank.

liaison officer at Salina Convent what was up with the Romanian border guards. They had turned hostile in the neighbouring sector. Two German groups of the company at the unit boundary had been overwhelmed by Russians or Romanians in a manner still uncertain,

A heavy 15-cm field howitzer of 3rd Mountain Division west of Suha in the Carpathians, summer 1944.

> and the Romanians had also fired flares which were answered from the Soviet front. Oberleutnant Kaack passed this information forward to division and promised the battalion that he would personally request the explanation from the Romanian brigade HQ. Then the telephone line went dead and contact to 'Lise' at Salina Convent was lost.[1]

That night 3rd Mountain Division lost three officers, thirty NCOs and 243 men who had been in the Romanian central sector. The Romanians tied up their former German and Austrian comrades and handed them over to the Soviets.

Generalmajor Klatt drew the necessary conclusions from the conduct of the Romanians. His immediate priority now was to erect a cohesive front in his own sector. On 25 August 1st

1. Klatt, *Die 3. Gebirgsdivision 1939–1945*, p. 284.

A mountain gun in firing position near Draceni.

Battalion, 144th Mountain Rifle Regiment, attacked the Romanian backsliders who were gathering at Gainesti and Salina Convent. Fleeing back to Valea Seaca they ran into Soviet troops and were taken prisoner. In that way the Romanians shared the fate of the German/Austrian brothers-in-arms they had betrayed.

3rd Mountain Division received orders from Army Group South Ukraine to prevent the Soviet breakthrough attempts on the pass

At the Kishinev market in Bessarabia.

A Gebirgsjäger *and a Romanian soldier haggling in the market.*

road and push back the Soviets by stages. In the early morning of 28 August 1944 2nd Battalion, 144th Mountain Rifle Regiment, again under Major Kloss, which until then had been protecting the road over the Aurel Pass to Borca, attacked northwards from the Gura-Largu area. Soviet units had penetrated the mountains there and were making occasional attempts to cut off 3rd Mountain Division. When Major Kloss reached Gura-Largu, he ran into enemy units which divided his battalion into two halves. Unaware of this he made a massive attack on the enemy.

In this nerve-racking fighting on a day in which the battalion advanced four kilometres (2.5 miles), it was especially sniper Matthäus Hetzenauer who helped the German bases at the Pluton Pass out of a crisis situation. This all counted towards his award of the Knight's Cross described later in the narrative.

Hetzenauer worked in company with the snipers Josef Allerberger and Josef Roth and many unknown *Gebirgsjäger*, with a very real fear of death, against a numerically superior enemy, for the pitiless duel with Soviet snipers knew no limits. No quarter was given by either side. Whoever had scruples and was nervous here had already lost and had little time to live.

At all the 3rd Mountain Division hotspots Hetzenauer met up with sniper Josef Allerberger. 'At the focal point of all our battles,' Allerberger stated,

> I made my appearance and forced the enemy on the defensive by my almost infallible shooting. My nerves were of steel. I knew this for sure as each projectile found its way with deadly certainty into the Russian ranks. In these desperate encounters it gave us the edge if we could undermine the enemy's fighting spirit. The experienced sniper aimed less for fatal hits than for hits to the torso, which put a man out of action and left him screaming in agony. This also significantly increased the number of hits in the heat of battle, and with this rapid rate of fire the screams of the seriously wounded demoralised their comrades and interrupted the momentum of the attack.

A Gebirgsjäger *radio NCO awaiting the order to advance.*

> The scheme of a Russian attack was to send forward four waves of troops, the rear two waves having no weapons. As the front two waves were cut down, the rear waves picked up the weapons of their dead and wounded. I developed my own response to perfection. I would bide my time until the four waves were on their way towards our lines, then open rapid fire into the two rear waves aiming for each target's stomach. The unexpected casualties at the rear and the terrible cries of the most seriously wounded tended to collapse the rear lines and so disconcert the two leading ranks that the whole attack would begin to falter.
>
> At this point I could now concentrate on the two leading waves, despatching those Soviets closer than fifty metres with a shot to the heart or head. Enemy soldiers who had turned and run I transformed into men screaming in agony with a shot to the kidneys. At this, an attack would frequently disintegrate altogether.
>
> In such an engagement I would often fire off more than twenty rounds, none of which counted towards my final total of successful shots.[1]

In this sector of the Eastern Front in particular, the many first-rate snipers of 3rd Mountain Division inflicted heavy losses on the Soviets. The Red Army troops, unused to fighting in mountainous terrain, were never able to penetrate the narrow, sealed passes of the *Gebirgsjäger* anywhere. The enemy assault parties, repeatedly repulsed, retreated to the dense mountain woodlands below and were shot by the snipers like game.

> The word 'shot' automatically brings to mind comparisons with the hunt and shocks many people nowadays [wrote Karl Ruef in his chronicle of 3rd Mountain Division], but whatever the reason for it, war is an ugly and brutal business, therefore many of its expressions are also brutal, but whoever fails to defend himself, goes under.

1. Wacker, *Sniper on the Eastern Front*, p. 18–19.

General Klatt (left) with Major von Aigner and Major Mansbart in Hungary, December 1944.

Dropping a bomb on a town, firing a heavy gun, loosing off a torpedo and so on is not so dangerous for the attacker, but still mostly lethal for those who get in the way. In the final analysis there was no difference for the recipient of the 'shot' of the sniper, who did not fire indiscriminately. The sniper was obliged to attack his target in the manner prescribed by Army regulations, his target being enemy artillery observers, officers, message runners, the crews of heavy guns and so on. The intent was not to kill people indiscriminately, but to eliminate those persons on the enemy side who represented a danger to one's own troops.

The sniper watched over the men in his own unit from an isolated position, protecting them against surprises. His accurate occasional rounds hampered bridge-building by pioneers, as Gefreiter Hetzenauer did for a whole day. And Obergefreiter Allerberger not only pinned down a Russian company, but inflicted such losses upon

Mountain artillery being towed by half-tracks on the move from Nagy-Banja to Szatmanemti for the Battle of Nyiregyhaza in October 1944.

it that the Red soldiers fled in panic, creating time for a German dressing station with twenty-seven wounded to be evacuated.

At the end of August when a Soviet attack over the northern flank of the Pluton Pass put the defenders of the Bistritz Valley in extreme danger, Hetzenauer took out thirty-eight Red soldiers in two days.

The sniper always had an observer with him. He lay well camouflaged and motionless for hours, mostly ahead of his own front line, constantly in danger of discovery by an enemy sniper. 'Just once I raised a foot a little from sheer boredom,' Allerberger recounted, 'and immediately a bullet went through the heel of the boot.' Many snipers fell or were seriously wounded.[1]

On 1 September 1944 Hetzenauer and all other Wehrmacht snipers were awarded the Iron Cross, Second Class, to compensate

1. Ruef, Karl, *Odyssee einer Gebirgsdivision. Die 3. Gebirgsdivision im Einsatz*, Graz and Stuttgart, 1976, p. 527*f*.

Obergefreiter Goller waits for General Paul Klatt to mount up.

them for having all their confirmed hits to that date written off at the introduction of the Sniper Badge.

Oberleutnant Bogenrieder leading 1st Company, 83rd Mountain Pioneer Battalion, clung doggedly to the rocky spot height 1440 north-east of Tarcasa in a bitter fight against a numerically far superior Soviet force and thus prevented the enemy from entering Bistritz Valley. Generalmajor Paul Klatt sent quickly formed battle groups including his snipers into the thick of the fighting to support Bogenrieder. They tied down the enemy, inflicting heavy losses.

Bogenrieder's pioneers were there to block off the Bistritz Valley. They blew up walls of rock, which then thundered down over the Carpathian mountain roads. This did not quite stop the fast advance of the Red Army but made its progress more difficult, thus allowing the *Gebirgsjäger* to find better defensive positions from which to continue the fight or, if time allowed, to set up a secured front line. Between 19 and 21 September 1944 the entire Soviet 42nd Guards Rifle Division attacked these new positions. Red Army tanks rolled along both sides of the road to Deda, but even this time Klatt and his commanders arranged their weak forces so skilfully that they took the enemy under flanking fire from the heights.

Two Red Army regiments had gone around the right flank of 3rd Mountain Division. On the night of 24 September 3rd Mountain Division pulled back to previously prepared positions west of Poleti. Three days later Klatt arrived at the command centre of Hungarian Colonel von Ferenczy just as it was surprised by the Red Army. Klatt's defence was successful and the enemy was repulsed. This achievement in the Deda area was mentioned in the Wehrmacht bulletin of 4 October 1944:

> In the fighting for Transylvania, the Austrian 3rd Mountain Division together with Silesian riflemen and Hungarian border protection units led by Knight's Cross holder Generalmajor Klatt, and the Württemberg-Baden 23rd Panzer Division led by Generalmajor von Radowitz, have especially distinguished themselves both in attack and defence.[1]

The German withdrawal began on 8 October 1944. Upon receipt of the code-word *Winterfest* the 3rd Mountain Division command post was transferred from Felsö-Repa to Bistritz, and from there to Bethen. During the strenuous marches of the coming weeks, in which defensive fighting flared up repeatedly, Generalmajor Klatt was in close touch with almost all sections under his command. He wrote of them:

> I was able to convince myself, after all that the infantry had achieved in the struggle behind us in the very difficult conditions of mountain warfare, of their intrepid and steadfast bearing . . . Once again the snipers Hetzenauer, Leopold Meier (who later fell at Seibusch in Slovakia), Josef Roth and Josef Allerberger had distinguished themselves.

On 24 October 1944, Eighth Army combined all its forces into an attack spearhead heading westwards for Nyiregyhaza. On the

1. *Die Berichte des OKW 1939–1945*, Munich, 2004, Vol. 5, p. 332.

evening of the 25th, Generalmajor Klatt gave the order to attack. In the early hours of the following day he joined the attacking battalions.

The course of immediately subsequent events is extracted from a daily situation report of 3rd Mountain Division to IX Army Corps dated 26 October 1944.

> 1. Southern Front (Group *Schassner*) fought off two attacks at 0900 and 1400 hrs mounted in divisional strength, both preceded by artillery fire in salvoes and mortars. A coordinated artillery barrage inflicted heavy losses on the enemy infantry and three tanks were destroyed. From around midday this sector defended against scattered enemy columns of various strengths which had reached the Nagykallo–Ujfeherto road on a broad front and were attempting to break through to the south and south-east. At the western end of Nagykallo a defensive front with heavy weapons was set up and 2nd Battalion, 91st Mountain Rifle Regiment, occupied the area west of Nagykallo. 1015th Tank Hunter Company was attached to Group *Schassner*.
> 2. With 144th Mountain Rifle Regiment, plus 138th Mountain Rifle Regiment less its 1st Battalion, the attack to the north-west was commenced at 0600 hrs. The first successes were obtained by the mass of V Cavalry Corps facing the enemy. The attack battalions, closed up tightly, obtained complete surprise with hardly a round fired and overran the enemy positions, afterwards reaching with relative ease the western edge of the great forest. The enemy was put to flight in panic leaving behind all his heavy weapons and communications equipment. Shortly after reaching the western edge of the woods our attack encountered massed columns of enemy troops advancing from Nyiregyhaza to the south-east. While some sections bore away to the south, the enemy confronted our attack group with a strong defensive front consisting especially of anti-tank guns, other heavy infantry weapons and

Slovakian border guards in the Carpathians, autumn 1944.

tanks. Against this strong enemy our attack came to a standstill in the midday hours principally because our own assault guns had to be pulled out on account of the enemy anti-tank gun front.

After amalgamation of all our heavy weapons and numbers of artillery batteries the attack was resumed at 1400 hrs. In bitter and tenacious fighting, with heavy losses on both sides, half of the attack group reached Szakut and made contact with elements of 23rd Panzer Division. A figure has not yet been put to the heavy enemy casualties and the large number of captured heavy weapons, vehicles and horses. Six enemy tanks were destroyed.

3. On combing through the battle area, our forces found mutilated civilians and women raped by the enemy at several locations. The division reports a number of especially serious cases as follows:

'On 25 October 1944 *Gebirgsjäger* of 1st Battalion, 144th Mountain Rifle Regiment (Kloss) during a cleansing operation at a vineyard in the Ardany Erdö area came across a totally distraught Hungarian found crouching at the entrance to an earth bunker. Our troops saw inside it the body of the Hungarian's murdered wife. She had been cut open from throat to lower abdomen. An unborn child had been beheaded. At Napkor a woman was raped by twenty Red Army soldiers, at Czukor a seventeen-year old girl was raped one after another by thirteen Red Army soldiers. At Nyiregyhaza the wife of an innkeeper died after being raped eighteen times.[1] At Nagykallo Russian tanks fired on fleeing civilian refugees. German prisoners here had been tortured and shot dead.

4. Departed: Regimental Group *Schassner* with 1st and 3rd Battalion, 91st Mountain Rifle Regiment, Reconnaissance Company, 8th SS Cavalry Division, 1st Battalion, 138th Mountain Rifle Regiment, 4th Battalion, 94th Mountain Artillery Regiment.

Signed, v. Eimannsberger[2]

There now followed for sniper Matthäus Hetzenauer and his comrades-in-arms the defensive fighting west of the Theiss and at Miskolc which lasted from 1 November until 3 December 1944. Until the further withdrawal to the Theiss front could begin, the divisional staff of 3rd Mountain Division remained for two days with elements of the division at Nyiregyhaza, and the Theiss was crossed on the night of 1 November in rain and snow, the temperature falling to -10°C. The German casualties in these defensive battles were high.

---

1. This horrific incident was witnessed by sniper Allerberger from a well-camouflaged hide. After the gang rape, the woman was killed by having a flare fired into her body through her vagina. When he saw a scouting party from his battalion approaching, he drew their attention to the incident by shooting dead the Russian officer and an NCO. As a result, all twenty-three Soviet participants in the atrocity were gunned down. Wacker, Albrecht, *Sniper on the Eastern Front*, pp. 115–17.
2. Klatt, *Die 3. Gebirgsdivision 1939–1945*, p. 306*f.*

Improvised protective pens for horse-drawn carts.

The Wehrmacht bulletin for 5 November 1944 included an additional report: 'In the area of Eastern Hungary the Austrian 3rd Mountain Division commanded by Generalmajor Klatt broke up a massive encirclement attempt by the enemy and distinguished itself by outstanding bravery (Battle of Nyiregyhaza).'[1]

On 6 November 1944 Matthäus Hetzenauer received a head wound from shrapnel but remained with his company. He was awarded the Black Wound Badge three days later. On 13 November 1944 he was awarded the Infantry Assault Badge in Silver. On 25 November 1944 Hetzenauer was awarded the Iron Cross, First Class, and on 3 December 1944 the Sniper Badge in Gold. Miskolc had to be abandoned on 3 December before the weak German security force was surrounded by the Red Army in the north and west.

1. *Die Berichte des OKW 1939–1945*, Munich 2004, Vol. 5, p. 384.

Heading towards defeat: an infantryman who knew how to make do.

As to the continuation of the fighting during the retreat of 3rd Mountain Division up to the exit from Hungary, General Klatt wrote:

> I had had to command XXIX Army Corps myself temporarily within earshot of an artillery battle. I had no ambition to command such a large unit, I preferred to remain with a division with which I could feel a closer affinity. About eight Soviet divisions were attacking on both sides of the Sajo, and with our reduced force it was not always possible to prevent them making deep inroads. It took a lot of effort and trouble to close off the gaps, and even then poorly. A decisive breakthrough on the right of the division occurred at Grosssteffelsdorf. At the time I was with my neighbour whose weak security

force, a Turkmenistani battalion, was in the process of evacuating its positions. These events occurred in mid-December . . .

We built a new front on the extensive ridge between Balog and Sajo, but the situation remained very much in the balance. Major attacks were fought off between 10 and 25 December and close-combat actions occurred repeatedly, even in the battery positions. Our thoughts in those fateful days went not only to our families at home but also to the Ardennes where on 16 December powerful Panzer forces had attacked the Americans and British. Despite initial successes the offensive eventually failed for shortage of fuel. Many people cherished the childish hope that we might still build a common front with our Western enemies in order to forestall the expected Soviet push into the heart of Europe.

At Budapest the situation was desperate, the Soviets completing their encirclement of the city on Christmas evening. The terrain we held was mountainous and thickly wooded, suitable for our method of fighting, delaying resistance. That is not to say that we were prepared for a retreat, and did not want to maintain our tactical position; numerous actions and counter-attacks bore witness to that.

On New Year's Day 1945 an operation commanded by Major Denk, 1st Battalion, 138th Mountain Rifle Regiment, was a total success as mentioned in the Wehrmacht bulletin of 2 January 1945. The still available daily divisional reports to corps of 1 January 1945 of another operation and of a fight with partisans on 3 January 1945 give more details.[1]

The 3rd Mountain Division retreat into Slovakia was now fought against Soviet elite divisions and partisans. Fighting in the valley of the Gran lasted until 9 February 1945. As can be seen from the documents reproduced in the plates pages recommending

1. Klatt, *Die 3. Gebirgs-Division 1939–1945*, p. 314.

A pre-war photograph. From the right, Ferdinand Schörner, Ludwig Schulz, an unknown officer and Karl von Le Suire.

Matthäus Hetzenauer for the award of the Knight's Cross of the Iron Cross, it was on 2 February 1945 in the Gran Valley[1] that the incident occurred upon which the award was based. The Knight's Cross was normally awarded only to officers and NCOs for personal bravery of the highest degree and for an outstanding contribution of strategic importance. The short recommendation reads:

> Gefreiter Hetzenauer has distinguished himself as a sniper by especially outstanding dynamism and dare-devil aggression. In the period from 1 September 1944 to 10 March 1945 he obtained 172 confirmed sniper hits. H., a simple modest soldier, fights daily unsupervised on

1. Hetzenauer's regimental comrade, sniper Sepp Allerberger, stated that, by the end of January 1945, 144th Mountain Rifle Regiment had retreated to the Gran River running through the great valley between the Erzgebirge mountains and Lower Tatra. Here, Sixth Army was attempting to re-form its forces to contain the Soviet pressure along its sector of the front. Wacker, *Sniper on the Eastern Front*, p. 120.

> his own initiative with unparalleled bravery, tirelessly and without regard to the constantly threatening danger to his life, and is known throughout the division for his fearless adventures as a lone soldier. H. obtained most of his hits by settling in ahead of our own main front line and immediately in front of the enemy positions and sought out his victims there without regard to our own or enemy artillery fire, or enemy attacks or assault troop operations. Thus on 2 February 1945, alone during an enemy attack operation, once again lying low before the enemy positions, he scored eighteen sniper hits. The overall result thereof was that H. put two tactically strong enemy companies out of action by himself and by his own intervention accomplished a success beyond the limits of his own sphere of activity.

The recommendation was signed by Generalleutnant Klatt, and endorsed by the corps' commanding general, Karl von Le Suire.

After 9 February 1945, 144th Mountain Rifle Regiment headed for the Waag Valley. Here XLIX Mountain Corps under General Karl von Le Suire had a command post west of Rosenberg, and at Rosenberg barracks Generalleutnant Klatt welcomed the 'Gneisenau Wave', a fresh regiment of reinforcements. Enemy attacks which began on 11 February were held off for three days, and on 14 February 3rd Mountain Division was mentioned in the Wehrmacht bulletin:

> In Slovakia strong enemy attacks were beaten off in fierce mountain fighting and some breakthroughs sealed off. This was a special defensive success for 3rd Mountain Division.[1]

A few days later Generalleutnant Klatt was informed that 3rd Mountain Division was to be relieved, and on 18 February 1945 the difficult withdrawal began over the deep snows of the Jublanka Pass into the Wesbeskides. From there the trail led north into the upper valley of the Vistula and on to Bielitz in Poland.

1. *Die Berichte des OKW*, Vol. 5, p. 523.

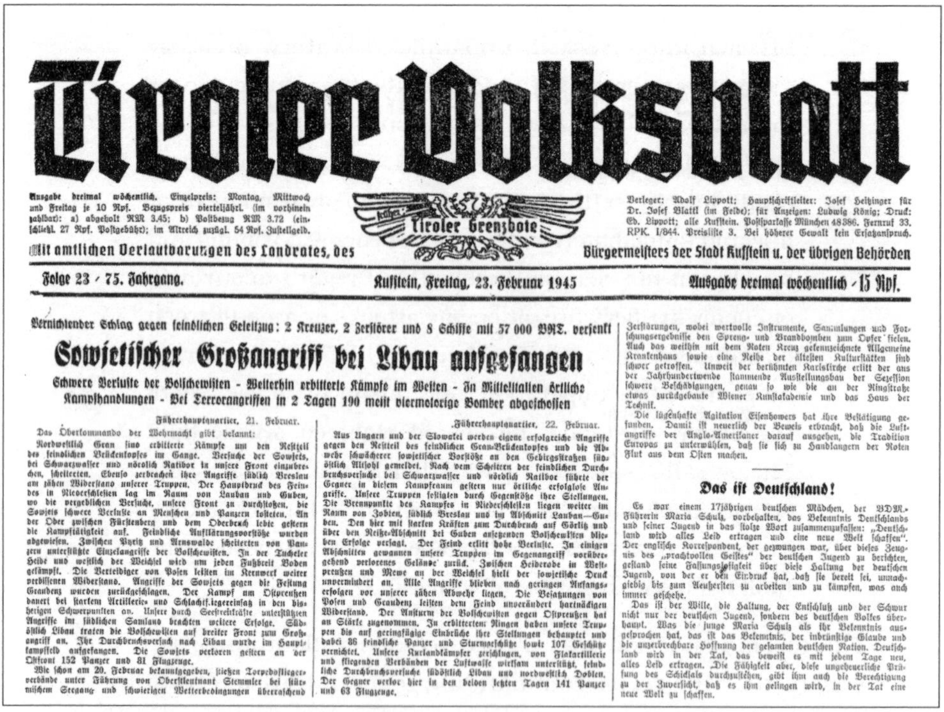

Tiroler Volksblatt

Ausgabe dreimal wöchentlich. Einzelpreis: Montag, Mittwoch und Freitag je 10 Rpf. Bezugspreis vierteljährl. (im vorhinein zahlbar): a) abgeholt RM 3.45; b) Postbezug RM 3.72 (einschließl. 27 Rpf. Postgebühr); im Altreich zuzügl. 54 Rpf. Zustellgeld.

Verleger: Adolf Lippott; Hauptschriftleiter: Josef Heitzinger für Dr. Josef Blattl (im Felde); für Anzeigen: Ludwig König; Druck: Ed. Lippott; alle Kufstein. Postsparkasse München 48386. Fernruf 33. RPK. I/844. Preisliste 3. Bei höherer Gewalt kein Ersatzanspruch.

Mit amtlichen Verlautbarungen des Landrates, des Bürgermeisters der Stadt Kufstein u. der übrigen Behörden

Folge 23 · 75. Jahrgang. — Kufstein, Freitag, 23. Februar 1945 — Ausgabe dreimal wöchentlich · 15 Rpf.

Vernichtender Schlag gegen feindlichen Geleitzug: 2 Kreuzer, 2 Zerstörer und 8 Schiffe mit 57 000 BRT. versenkt

Sowjetischer Großangriff bei Libau aufgefangen

Schwere Verluste der Bolschewisten - Weiterhin erbitterte Kämpfe im Westen - In Mittelitalien örtliche Kampfhandlungen - Bei Terrorangriffen in 2 Tagen 190 meist viermotorige Bomber abgeschossen

Führerhauptquartier, 21. Februar.

Das Oberkommando der Wehrmacht gibt bekannt:

Nordwestlich Gran sind erbitterte Kämpfe um den Restteil des feindlichen Brückenkopfes im Gange. Versuche der Sowjets, bei Schwarzwasser und nördlich Ratibor in unsere Front einzubrechen, scheiterten. Ebenso zerbrachen ihre Angriffe südlich Breslau am zähen Widerstand unserer Truppen. Der Hauptdruck des Feindes in Niederschlesien lag im Raum von Lauban und Guben, wo die vergeblichen Versuche, unsere Front zu durchstoßen, die Sowjets schwere Verluste an Menschen und Panzern kosteten. An der Oder zwischen Fürstenberg und dem Oderbruch lebte gestern die Kampftätigkeit auf. Feindliche Aufklärungsvorstöße wurden abgewiesen. Zwischen Pyritz und Arnswalde scheiterten von Panzern unterstützte Einzelangriffe der Bolschewisten. In der Tucheler Heide und westlich der Weichsel wird um jeden Fußbreit Boden gekämpft. Die Verteidiger von Posen leisten im Kernwerk weiter verbissenen Widerstand. Angriffe der Sowjets gegen die Festung Graudenz wurden zurückgeschlagen. Der Kampf um Ostpreußen dauert bei starkem Artillerie- und Schlachtfliegereinsatz in den bisherigen Schwerpunkten an. Unsere durch Seestreitkräfte unterstützten Angriffe im südlichen Samland brachten weitere Erfolge. Südöstlich Libau traten die Bolschewisten auf breiter Front zum Großangriff an. Ihr Durchbruchsversuch nach Libau wurde im Hauptkampffeld aufgefangen. Die Sowjets verloren gestern an der Ostfront 152 Panzer und 81 Flugzeuge.

Wie schon am 20. Februar bekanntgegeben, stießen Torpedofliegerverbände unter Führung von Oberstleutnant Stemmler bei stürmischem Seegang und schwierigen Wetterbedingungen überraschend

Führerhauptquartier, 22. Februar.

Aus Ungarn und der Slowakei werden eigene erfolgreiche Angriffe gegen den Restteil des feindlichen Gran-Brückenkopfes und die Abwehr schwächerer sowjetischer Vorstöße an den Gebirgsstraßen südöstlich Altsohl gemeldet. Nach dem Scheitern der feindlichen Durchbruchsversuche bei Schwarzwasser und nördlich Ratibor führte der Gegner in diesem Kampfraum gestern nur örtliche erfolglose Angriffe. Unsere Truppen festigten durch Gegenstöße ihre Stellungen. Die Brennpunkte des Kampfes in Niederschlesien liegen weiter im Raum von Zobten, südlich Breslau und im Abschnitt Lauban—Guben. Den hier mit starken Kräften zum Durchbruch auf Görlitz und über den Neiße-Abschnitt bei Guben ansetzenden Bolschewisten blieben Erfolge versagt. Der Feind erlitt hohe Verluste. In einigen Abschnitten gewannen unsere Truppen im Gegenangriff vorübergehend verlorenes Gelände zurück. Zwischen Heiderode in Westpreußen und Mewe an der Weichsel hielt der sowjetische Druck unvermindert an. Alle Angriffe blieben nach geringen Anfangserfolgen vor unserer zähen Abwehr liegen. Die Besatzungen von Posen und Graudenz leisten dem Feind unverändert hartnäckigen Widerstand. Der Ansturm der Bolschewisten gegen Ostpreußen hat an Stärke zugenommen. In erbitterten Ringen haben unsere Truppen bis auf geringfügige Einbrüche ihre Stellungen behauptet und dabei 86 feindliche Panzer und Sturmgeschütze sowie 107 Geschütze vernichtet. Unsere Kurlandkämpfer zerschlugen, von Flakartillerie und fliegenden Verbänden der Luftwaffe wirksam unterstützt, feindliche Durchbruchsversuche südöstlich Libau und nordwestlich Doblen. Der Gegner verlor hier in den beiden letzten Tagen 141 Panzer und 63 Flugzeuge.

Zerstörungen, wobei wertvolle Instrumente, Sammlungen und Forschungsergebnisse den Spreng- und Brandbomben zum Opfer fielen. Auch das weithin mit dem Roten Kreuz gekennzeichnete Allgemeine Krankenhaus sowie eine Reihe der ältesten Kulturstätten sind schwer getroffen. Unweit der berühmten Karlskirche erlitt der aus der Jahrhundertwende stammende Ausstellungsbau der Sezession schwere Beschädigungen, genau so wie die an der Ringstraße etwas zurückgebaute Wiener Kunstakademie und das Haus der Technik.

Die lügenhafte Agitation Eisenhowers hat ihre Bestätigung gefunden. Damit ist neuerlich der Beweis erbracht, daß die Luftangriffe der Anglo-Amerikaner darauf ausgehen, die Tradition Europas zu unterwühlen, daß sie sich zu Handlangern der Roten Flut aus dem Osten machen.

Das ist Deutschland!

Es war einem 17jährigen deutschen Mädchen, der BDM.-Führerin Maria Schulz, vorbehalten, das Bekenntnis Deutschlands und seiner Jugend in das stolze Wort zusammenzufassen: „Deutschland wird alles Leid ertragen und eine neue Welt schaffen". Der englische Korrespondent, der gezwungen war, über dieses Zeugnis des „prachtvollen Geistes" der deutschen Jugend zu berichten, gestand seine Fassungslosigkeit über diese Haltung der deutschen Jugend, von der er den Eindruck hat, daß sie bereit sei, unnachgiebig bis zum Aeußersten zu arbeiten und zu kämpfen, was auch immer geschehe.

Das ist der Wille, die Haltung, der Entschluß und der Schwur nicht nur der deutschen Jugend, sondern des deutschen Volkes überhaupt. Was die junge Maria Schulz als ihr Bekenntnis ausgesprochen hat, das ist das Bekenntnis, der inbrünstige Glaube und die unzerbrechbare Hoffnung der gesamten deutschen Nation. Deutschland wird in der Tat, das beweist es mit jedem Tage neu, alles Leid ertragen. Die Fähigkeit aber, diese ungeheuerliche Prüfung des Schicksals durchzustehen, gibt ihm auch die Berechtigung zu der Zuversicht, daß es ihm gelingen wird, in der Tat eine neue Welt zu schaffen.

Front page of the Tiroler Volksblatt, *23 February 1945.*

Matthäus Hetzenauer had been interviewed by his local press before the award of his Knight's Cross, and the 23 February 1945 edition of *Tiroler Volksblatt* published at Kufstein began its coverage by quoting from an official report:

> '. . . several snipers, amongst them Gefreiter Hetzenauer serving with a Steiermark *Gebirgsjäger* regiment and credited with 92 hits, who has distinguished himself with especially good shooting.'

This extract from a January 1945 Wehrmacht bulletin conceals behind the statistic a high degree of skill, bravery and prudent planning which bear no relationship to the sober manner of reporting it. Iron Crosses of both classes, the letter of recognition with a photograph of his divisional commander, the sniper certificate with praise from the army commander – these all underline the outstanding achievement of this sniper.

23. Februar 1945 „Tiroler Volksblatt"

Aus Stadt und Land

Für Deutschland gefallen

Im Kampf um Deutschlands Freiheit starben in treuer Pflichterfüllung den Heldentod:

Kufstein: Leutnant und Kompanieführer Pg. Walter Wiendl Inhaber des Eisernen Kreuzes 2. Klasse, 21 Jahre alt, im Osten.

Kirchbichl: Gefreiter Georg Wiedmann, Reichsbahnangestellter, im Nordabschnitt der Ostfront.

Kramsach: Gefreiter in einem Gebirgsjäger-Regiment Alois Hirzinger, Inhaber des Eisernen Kreuzes 2. Klasse, 20 Jahre alt, im Westen. — Gebirgsjäger Anton Horngacher, Bauer beim Hansiger, 37 Jahre alt, in Ungarn.

Wildschönau: Oberjäger Michael Schoner, Inhaber des Eisernen Kreuzes 2. Klasse, Teilnehmer an den Feldzügen in Norwegen, Finnland und im Westen, 27 Jahre alt, im Westen.

Ihr Opfertod ist uns Verpflichtung zu höchstem Einsatz!

Ein Scharfschütze

NSG. „Mehrere Scharfschützen, darunter der Gefreite Hetzenauer in einem steierischen Gebirgsjäger-Regiment mit 92 Abschüssen, zeichneten sich durch besondere gute Schußleistungen aus." Diese Ergänzung zu einem Wehrmachtbericht vom November v. J. verbirgt hinter der Nennung einer Zahl ein Beträchtliches an Geschick, Tapferkeit und Ueberlegenheit, die in keinem Verhältnis zu der sachlichen Nüchternheit ihrer Satzgebung stehen. Die Eisernen Kreuze beider Klassen, das Anerkennungsschreiben mit einem Bild seines Divisionskommandeurs, die Scharfschützenurkunde mit einer Belobung durch den Armeeführer — das alles unterstreicht die hervorragende Leistung dieses Scharfschützen, der nun bald — es ist inzwischen draußen schon dämmrig geworden — von seinem täglichen „Jagdgang" im Gefechtsstand zurückerwartet wird.

Hetzenauer, knapp 10 Monate Soldat, eröffnete einen Tag nach seiner Rückkehr vom Heimaturlaub — er stammt aus einem der einsamen Bergbauernhöfe bei Brixen im Tale im Kreise Kitzbühel — das neue Jahr mit drei weiteren Abschüssen. Inzwischen hat er die Zahl auf 119 erhöht, und das in einer Gesamtzeit von kaum 5 Monaten. Dies bedeutet — einen Monat Marschbewegungen und einen weiteren des Urlaubs abgerechnet — im Durchschnitt jeden Tag mindestens einen abgeschossenen und für den Feind ausgefallenen Bolschewisten."

„Gefreiter Hetzenauer heute drei Bolschewisten außer Verpflegung gesetzt!" Mit dieser ihm geläufigsten humoristischen Formulierung meldet sich der Gefreite bei seinem Kompaniechef im Gefechtsstand zurück und hat damit heute seine Gesamtabschußzahl auf 122 gesteigert. Diese Art der Meldung ist bezeichnend für den kaum zwanzigjährigen, schlanken und hochgewachsenen Tiroler Jäger, hinter dessen bescheidener Wesensart und überlegener Ruhe Blick und Haltung unschwer den geborenen Scharfschützen erkennen lassen. Der Aufforderung, etwas Ausführliches, irgendwelche besonderen Erlebnisse aus seinen verschiedenen Einsätzen zu schildern, kommt H. nur zögernd nach, seine eigenen Erfolge scheinen ihm zu selbstverständlich, um sie noch besonders zu erwähnen. Nur ein kleines Erlebnis weiß er zu berichten, und auch dieses wahrscheinlich nur deshalb, weil er damals — in den schweren Kämpfen um Miscolc — es mit zwei Feinden „vom Fach" zu tun hatte, zwei bolschewistischen Scharfschützen, die er erst nach längerem, wechselreichem Feuergefecht dann schließlich doch noch „außer Verpflegung setzen" konnte. Von der Mühe und Ausdauer, die es oftmals erforderlich machen, Stunde um Stunde in jeder Witterung, mitunter tagelang vergeblich vor einem gut getarnten Gegner zu liegen, ohne zum Schuß zu kommen — davon erwähnt H. nichts. Während der Unterhaltung widmet er seine ganze Aufmerksamkeit seinem ihm zu einem Begriff höchster Kostbarkeit gewordenen Scharfschützengewehr.

Einmal, als Hetzenauer für kurze Zeit den Gefechtsstand verließ, berichtete sein Kompaniechef von einem gelungenen Abschuß der letzten Tage: Hetzenauer habe mit einem zweiten Scharfschützen vor einem sowjetischen MG. gelegen, neben dem sich zwei Bolschewisten eben ihre Zigaretten anzündeten. Darauf hätte H. zu seinem Kameraden gesagt: „So freche Hunde! Die lassen wir die halbe Zigarette noch rauchen, aber dann schnakelt's!" Auf ein verabredetes Zeichen hin „schnakelte" es dann auch wirklich, für die beiden Bolschewisten wurde es die letzte Zigarette!

Wenn im Wehrmachtbericht und in der Tagespresse gelegentlich auch der stolzenkämpferischen Leistungen und Erfolge der großdeutschen Gebirgsdivisionen Erwähnung getan wird, dann haben — gerade im gebirgsmäßigen Einsatz — einen erheblichen Anteil daran die Scharfschützen, die täglich in verbissener, beharrlicher Zähigkeit Abschuß auf Abschuß erzielen.

Soldatentod. Gefreiter Josef Götsch aus Kufstein ist an den Folgen einer in Finnland erworbenen Krankheit im Alter von 22 Jahren gestorben. — Gebirgsjäger Wilhelm Schwaiger aus Kufstein ist im Alter von 18 Jahren einem tragischen Unglücksfall erlegen.

Altersjubiläen. Am 16. Februar vollendete Frau Barbara Haberstroh, Endach 4, ihr 82. Lebensjahr. Sie stammt aus Oberhausen, kam 1896 nach Kufstein und ist die Witwe eines Maurers, dem sie zwei Töchter schenkte. Frau Haberstroh ist noch immer rüstig und nimmt am Zeitgeschehen regen Anteil. — Am 26. Februar vollenden Herr Johann Gaisbacher, Thierberg, das 82. und Frau Juliane Neuner, Kienbergstraße 5, das 79. Lebensjahr. Volksgenosse Gaisbacher war viele Jahre Triftmeister der Stadt Kufstein und hat bis ins hohe Alter hinein immer fleißig gearbeitet. Frau Neuner wohnt seit 1912 in Kufstein. Sie ist noch immer fleißig bei der Arbeit, spinnt Wolle und strickt daraus Socken und Handschuhe für ihre Enkel an der Front. Sie ist Mutter eines Sohnes und einer Tochter. — Allen Jubilaren die besten Glückwünsche!

Einkaufshilfe für Berufstätige. Eine praktische Hilfe für Berufstätige wurde in einer Stadt des Altreichs geschaffen, die wir zur Nachahmung empfehlen möchten. In allen Lebensmittelgeschäften wurden „Bestellkästen für berufstätige Frauen" angebracht, damit den Frauen, die neben der Arbeit noch ihren Haushalt versehen müssen, das lange Anstehen erspart bleibt. Sie stecken auf dem Wege zur Arbeit ihre „Wunschzettel" in den Bestellkasten, und der Kaufmann macht im Laufe des Tages alles zurecht, so daß die Frauen ihre Ware auf dem Nachhausewege ohne langes Warten in Empfang nehmen können. Mit dieser Einrichtung wird dem Kaufmann auch die gerechte Verteilung der Mangelware erleichtert.

Angath. Todesfall. Am 20. Februar starb im Alter von 73 Jahren Frau Katharina Weiskopf geborene Ehrenstraßer. Sie war die Ehefrau des Tischlermeisters Karl Weiskopf. Sie hinterläßt vier Söhne und zwei Töchter.

Brandenberg. Wir müssen und werden siegen. Die Partei rief die Volksgenossen zu einer öffentlichen Versammlung, in der nach Eröffnung durch Ortsgruppenleiter Pg. Schatz Reichsredner SA.-Obersturmführer Pg. Krucher sprach. Er hob den unzählige Male bekundeten und bewiesenen Friedenswillen des Führers und des deutschen Volkes hervor, im Gegensatz zum internationalen Judentum mit seinem Bestreben, das deutsche Volk mit allen Mitteln zu vernichten. Mit gespannter Aufmerksamkeit folgten die Versammelten den eindringlichen Worten des Redners, als er darauf hinwies, daß wir jetzt auf dem Höhepunkt des Kampfes stünden, daß der Gegner nun alles daransetze, um mit der Niederlage Deutschlands nicht nur jedem einzelnen von uns Verderben und Untergang, sondern auch der ganzen kultivierten und gesitteten Welt Vernichtung zu bereiten, daß wir siegen müssen, damit nicht alle schon gebrachten Opfer umsonst wären, und daß wir siegen werden, wenn jeder im Vertrauen auf den Führer sein Bestes leistet.

Kössen. Todesfall. Die Bäuerin zu Kleinschmied, Frau Marie Salvenmoser, ist am 19. Februar im Alter von 83 Jahren gestorben. Sie hinterläßt mit ihrem Ehemann drei Söhne und zwei Töchter.

Westendorf. Auszeichnung. Gefreiter Kaspar Aschaber wurde für besondere Tapferkeit vor dem Feinde in Ungarn mit dem Eisernen Kreuz 2. Klasse ausgezeichnet. Er ist Bauer zu Eckart. (o)

Westendorf. Hochzeit. Geheiratet haben der Bauer zu Daxenasten in der Windau Johann Jaß und die Bauerntochter zu Vordergetzen Katharina Hölzl. (o)

Standesamtliche Meldungen

Kufstein. Geboren wurden den Ehepaaren Anna und Josef Schmidbauer, Römerhofgasse 6, als 1. Kind ein Mädel Christine; Anna und Peter Blaickner, Breitenbach, Kleinsöll 2, als 12. Kind ein Junge Siegfried; Marie und Josef Weiß, Karl-Kraft-Straße 3, als 3. Kind ein Mädel Helga. Gestorben sind: Juliana Probst geborene Stempfer, Platz der SA., 61 Jahre; Veronika Fasser geborene Danzl, Kundl, Bahnhofstraße 185, 71 Jahre; Rudolf Neubacher, Innsbruck, 2 Jahre; Marie Wiedner geborene Hamberger, Innsbruck, 76 Jahre; Minna Mühlbauer geborene Hill, Degerndorf, 47 Jahre. (g)

Alpbach. Gestorben ist im Alter von 66 Jahren der Bauer Thomas Moser zu Unterblaicken 70.

Ebbs. Geboren wurde als 3. Kind der Familie Josef Beikircher, zu Dorf 45. (g)

Rattenberg. Geboren wurde als 3. Kind der Familie Marie Ascher, Inngasse 54. Gestorben sind Anna Payerl geborene Goldhammer, Bienerstraße 84, im Alter von 70 Jahren, sowie Lorenz Bliem, Bienerstraße 85, im Alter von 76 Jahren.

Reith bei Brixlegg. Im Jänner 1945 wurden geboren Inge Bilgeri als 3. Kind, sowie Adolf Mühlegger als 1. Kind.

Söll. Gestorben sind Anna Horngacher, Bromberg 40, 77 Jahre alt; Josef Maier, Stockach 65, 40 Jahre alt; Georg Sojer, Stockach 33, 64 Jahre alt.

On an inside page of the Tiroler Volksblatt, *Kufstein edition, of 23 February 1945 under the sub-heading* 'Ein Scharfschütze' *is the report of an interview with Matthäus Hetzenauer.*

Hetzenauer, barely ten months a soldier, opened the New Year with three more hits just a day after his return from home leave – he comes from one of the remote mountain farms at Brixen im Thale near Kitzbühel. Meanwhile his score has risen to 119, and that in a period of only five months. This means – allowing one month on the march and another month of leave – on average every day one shot Bolshevist lost to the enemy.

Dawn has already begun to break outside and he is expected to return to the command post from his daily 'hunt'. 'Gefreiter Hetzenauer has removed three more Bolshevists today from the rations list!' This is his humorous way of reporting his success to his company commander at the command post, and today his total number of hits has risen to 122. This way of reporting is characteristic of the slim and tall Tyrolean hunter, barely twenty years old, in whose modesty, calm gaze and deportment it is not difficult to recognise the born sniper.

To a request to describe at length some special experience from his various missions, Hetzenauer responds with hesitation, for his own successes seem to him to be too routine for special mention. He decides on a minor experience, and even this probably only because – in the heavy fighting at Miskolc – he tangled with two enemies 'of the trade', two Bolshevist snipers whom he removed 'from the rations list' only after a long exchange of fire. Of the effort and endurance which often make it necessary, hour after hour in all weathers, sometimes lying all day without a result opposite a well camouflaged enemy without ever firing – of that Hetzenauer says nothing. During our conversation he focussed all his attention on the most valuable thing in the world for him, his sniper's rifle.

Once when he left the command post for a short while his company commander talked about a recent successful shot; Hetzenauer lay with another sniper

Award of the Honour Scroll Bar to Hauptmann Völkl (right) on 6 January 1945.

facing a Soviet machine gun near which two Bolshevists lit up their cigarettes. 'Cheeky dogs! We'll let them smoke half and then snuff them out.' At the agreed sign they really were snuffed out, and for the two Bolshevists it was the last cigarette.

When the Wehrmacht bulletins and the daily newspapers make occasional mention of the proud successes of Greater Germany's mountain divisions, the snipers have – in mountain operations alone – a substantial share in them, scoring every day with dogged, unwavering, steadfast tenacity.

From 10 March 1945, 3rd Mountain Division was involved again in bitter fighting. The Sturmgeschütz assault guns under Knight's Cross holder Oberleutnant Holzinger attacked repeatedly and skilfully with success. On 21 March the *Bozner Tagblatt* reported:

> Strong Soviet forces attempted to break through to an important valley road to the west supported by 5,000 rounds of artillery fire. The enemy plan was thwarted in fierce mountain fighting. By evening all sections of the main front line were back in our hands. An alpine *Gebirgs*jäger regiment at the enemy attack strongpoint inflicted especially grievous losses on the Soviets, the enemy losing more than a hundred dead in a few hours. Often left to his own devices, the German *Gebirgsjäger* in this fight proved himself once again to be a fanatical lone soldier.

Of the eleven mountain divisions of the Wehrmacht – numbered 1–10 and 188 – the 3rd suffered the most casualties during the Second World War.

In order to encourage further the 'Soldiers in the East', on 15 April 1945 Hitler and Goebbels put together an Order of the Day as follows:

> Soldiers of the German Eastern Front! For the last time the Jewish-Bolshevist arch-enemy is attacking in masses. He is attempting to reduce Germany to rubble and exterminate our *Volk*. You soldiers in the East are already well aware what fate threatens above all our German women and children. While the aged, men and children will be murdered, women and maidens will be debased as barracks whores. Whoever remains will be marched off to Siberia.
>
> We saw this coming, and since January this year no effort has been spared in building a strong front. Powerful artillery will greet the enemy. Our losses in infantry have been made good by countless new battalions. Alarm units, new formations and *Volkssturm* are strengthening our front. The Bolshevik will this time experience the old fate of Asia and must be bled to death outside the capital of the German Reich.
>
> Whoever at this time fails to do his duty is a traitor to our *Volk*. The regiment or division which abandons

After the defection of Romania from the Axis in August 1944, 3rd Mountain Division on the move in the Bistrica Valley over the high pass to Borka.

> its positions acts dishonourably and will be shamed by the women and children who stand fast in our cities resisting the terrorist aerial bombers. Take notice above all of the few traitorous officers and men who in order to save their own miserable skins will fight against us in the pay of the Russians, perhaps even in German uniform. That person who, being unknown to you, gives orders to retreat, is to be arrested on the spot and if necessary executed forthwith irrespective of whatever rank he holds . . .

On this theme General Klatt's memoir also recorded:

> I must not forget to mention that at Putnok, a *Gebirgsjäger* captured by the Russians sent a letter to myself and the commander of 8th Jäger Division. It was written by Major Ott, commander of a battalion that had been wiped out at Miskolc in the Bükk mountains. The letter was cleverly worded and intended to convince us of the futility of fighting on.

> I met Major Ott after the capitulation in the PoW camp at Modra/Pressburg where he wore the black-white-red armband of the National Committee *Freies Deutschland*, and again he attempted to turn me on behalf of the Soviets. This was typical of the propaganda side of war which the Soviets made use of with all means in critical situations, by loudspeakers, aerial leaflets and so-called defectors or returners.[1]

Hitler's Order of the Day continued:

> If in the coming days and weeks every soldier on the Eastern Front does his duty, this final attack by Asia will be broken down just as, in the end and despite everything, a radical change will occur within our enemies in the West. Berlin will remain German, Vienna will be German again and Europe will never be Russian. Build a community sworn to defend not the empty concept of Fatherland, but your Homeland, your wives, children and with it our future!
>
> In this hour the German *Volk* looks to you, my fighters in the east, hoping only that your steadfastness, your fanaticism, your weaponry and leadership will bog down the Bolshevist assault in a bloodbath. At this very moment Fate has removed from the Earth the greatest war criminal of all times [meant here is US President Roosevelt, who died on 12 April 1945] and decided the turning point of the war . . .

1. Klatt, *Die 3. Gebirgs-Division 1939–1945*, p. 314.

Chapter 6

The Most Successful Wehrmacht Snipers

SHORTLY BEFORE HITLER'S Order of the Day to the 'Soldiers on the German Eastern Front', on 11 April 1945, Matthäus Hetzenauer was promoted to *Gefreiter*, and was then awarded the Knight's Cross of the Iron Cross on 17 April 1945 at regimental HQ Friedberg (Mährisch-Ostrau) as a sniper of 7th Company, 144th Mountain Rifle Regiment.

The rule was that a sniper required an independent witness for every claim, the entry then being made in his sniper's log. If the sniper was taking part in a German attack, or defending against an enemy attack, the results of his shooting did not count. For this reason the actual number of enemy soldiers killed by German sniper fire is at least twice that recorded for each man.

The most successful Wehrmacht snipers after 1 September 1944 were:

1. Matthäus Hetzenauer, 144th Mountain Rifle Regiment, 3rd Mountain Division, 346 credited
2. Josef Allerberger, 144th Mountain Rifle Regiment, 3rd Mountain Division, 257 credited
3. Bruno Sutkus, 196th Grenadier Regiment, 68th Infantry Division, 209 credited
4. Jakob Hechl, 91st Mountain Rifle Regiment, 4th Mountain Division, 121 credited
5. Helmut Wirnsberger, 3rd Mountain Division, 64 credited.

Matthäus Hetzenauer as a sniper with 3rd Mountain Division.

Albrecht Wacker in his biographical study of Josef Allerberger *Im Auge des Jägers* created a literary monument to the German sniper.

> The focal point of this work is a so-called 'sharpshooter', that kind of soldier to be found in the electrical field of admiration and disgust, overlooked and forgotten by war historians, who rendered outstanding service and often by his fearlessness and bravery saved the lives of many of his comrades-in-arms, while wiping out the life of an enemy with repeated startling precision. As few other soldiers had to, after the war snipers were forced to live with the burden of having extinguished many lives, not anonymously, but eye to eye with their opponents. Nearly all of them shut themselves off with this knowledge for the rest of their lives. Scarcely one of them is prepared to provide an unvarnished account.
>
> Josef 'Sepp' Allerberger was a carpenter's apprentice from near Salzburg in Austria, sucked into an ever smaller whirlpool of events on the Eastern Front in the first days of July 1943. From then until the end of the war, his life centred around his comrades and the fortunes of 144th Regiment, 3rd Mountain Division. The soldiers of this division were recruited mainly from the Austrian Alps. The ethnic consistency would be one of the major factors contributing to its high *esprit de corps*.[1]

The research of military author Oberst Karl Ruef proved by interviewing witnesses that Obergefreiter Allerberger was awarded the Knight's Cross by Generalfeldmarschall Schörner at Mönichshof on 20 April 1945 for 257 confirmed hits.[2]

Gefreiter Bruno Sutkus, a previously little known but nevertheless very successful Wehrmacht sniper, received at the year's end 1944 a formal letter recognising his high quota of hits from the commander-in-chief, 4th Panzer Army, to which the 68th Berlin-

1. Wacker, *Im Auge des Jägers*, p. 9.
2. Ruef, *Odyssee einer Gebirgsdivision, Die 3. Gebirgsdivision im Einsatz*, p. 527.

Brandenburg Infantry Division was attached at the time. As a member of 2nd Battalion, 196th Grenadier Regiment, he emerged victorious in sniper duels with Soviet sharpshooters 'decided in his favour by reason of his experience, his high degree of cunning, his patience and endurance and not least the necessary small quantum of luck'.[1]

Success in his objective required of the sniper not only an above-average level of marksmanship, but beyond that the maximum possible tactical skill together with patience and endurance. Perfect facial and body camouflage also played a role not to be underestimated and a considerable proportion of sniper training in the Seetaler Alps was dedicated to this.

Oberjäger[2] Jakob Hechl, although not featuring at the top of the list of the most successful snipers, has a special place amongst them for being decorated on 12 March 1945, therefore in the month before Matthäus Hetzenauer, with the Knight's Cross while serving with 3rd Company, 91st Mountain Rifle Regiment, 4th Mountain Division.

The standard work on the award, *Die Ritterkreuzträger 1939–1945*, states that his Knight's Cross 'cannot be substantiated at the Bundesarchiv',[3] and for this reason his name was left out of the index of Knight's Cross holders in the 4th Mountain Division military history.[4]

The *Bozener Tagblatt* edition of 18 April 1945, however, reported the award of the Knight's Cross to Hechl by Generalfeldmarschall Ferdinand Schörner as having been made at the Chemnitz military hospital. 'The Tyroleans have proven to have a sharp eye and steady hand,' the editorial stated. 'This sniper in a *Gebirgsjäger* regiment, with which he fought at the Kuban, in the Carpathians and Beskides as a proven scouting and assault party leader, recently obtained his 100th confirmed kill.'

1. Brookesmith, *Scharfschützen*, p. 58.
2. Equivalent to corporal.
3. Seemen, Gerhard von, *Die Ritterkreuzträger 1939–1945*, Friedberg, 1976, p. 379.
4. Kaltenegger, Roland, *Gebirgssoldaten unter dem Zeichen des 'Enzian': Schicksalsweg und Kampf der 4. Gebirgs-Division 1940–1945*, Graz & Stuttgart, 1983.

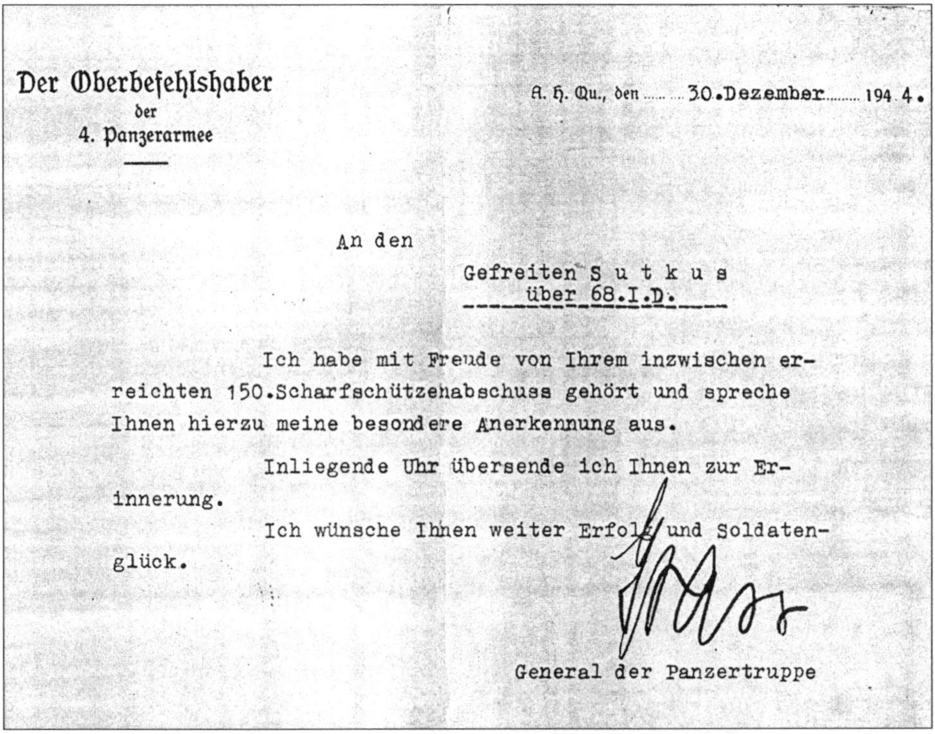

Der Oberbefehlshaber
der
4. Panzerarmee

A. H. Qu., den 30.Dezember 194 4.

An den

Gefreiten S u t k u s
über 68.I.D.

Ich habe mit Freude von Ihrem inzwischen erreichten 150.Scharfschützenabschuss gehört und spreche Ihnen hierzu meine besondere Anerkennung aus.

Inliegende Uhr übersende ich Ihnen zur Erinnerung.

Ich wünsche Ihnen weiter Erfolg und Soldatenglück.

General der Panzertruppe

The formal letter of recognition from General der Panzertruppe Fritz-Hubert Gräser, commanding Fourth Panzer Army, congratulating sniper Bruno Sutkus on his 150th confirmed kill and enclosing the gift of a watch.

On the basis of this report Jakob Hechl received his entry in the Tyrolean Book of Honour.[1] The text states that he was born on 10 June 1921 as one of the six children of Josef Hechl and Anna Hechl (*née* Rangger), innkeepers of the 'Kirchenwirt' at Vorder-Thiersee. After elementary school he worked on a farm until being conscripted into the military on 2 October 1940. He completed his basic training with 100th Mountain Rifle Reinforcement Battalion at Reichenhall, was sent to Russia with an infantry battalion and was wounded for the first time west of Dnepropetrovsk. After his recovery he was transferred into 4th Mountain Division. From then until the spring of 1945 he made 3rd Company, 91st Mountain Rifle Regiment, his military home.

1. Eppacher & Ruef, *Hohe Tapferkeitsauszeichnungen an Tiroler im Zweiten Weltkrieg*, p. 27.

A sketch showing a sharpshooter of the German mountain troops with sniper rifle.

Jakob Hechl experienced the fighting in the Caucasus, the Kuban bridgehead encirclement, the crossing into the Crimean peninsula, the fighting west of the Lower Dnieper, in Romania, eastern Hungary, in the Carpathians and in Upper Silesia. Merely by repeating the names of these theatres of war one sees an enormous quantity of individual fates, despair, bloody sacrifices and also intrepid service. Jakob Hechl belonged amongst the fearless, with the scouting and assault parties and the snipers.

Despite receiving a through-and-through wound to his lower leg on the Dnieper he was soon back with 3rd Company, 91st Mountain Rifle Regiment.

Hechl's total of confirmed hits as a sniper was 121 from 1 September 1944. By then he already had a series of decorations for bravery. On 12 March 1945 at Ratibor he was seriously wounded (shot in the head) and taken to the military hospital at Chemnitz. There he was visited in mid-April by Generalfeldmarschall Ferdinand Schörner and decorated with the Knight's Cross.

After the war Hechl had no certificate and so the sequence of events is not beyond dispute, but for those who know Ferdinand Schörner's method Hechl's claim appears to be absolutely credible. Moreover, Chemnitz was on the disputed demarcation line between Russians and Americans. It changed hands several times and on these occasions the patients at the military hospital were usually robbed. Jakob Hechl was eventually transferred from Chemnitz to the military hospital at Kreuznach-Biederstein and from there sent home as a seriously disabled ex-serviceman.

Gebirgsjäger Gerhard Muenke of 13th Mountain Rifle Regiment wrote of another 4th Mountain Division sniper in an article describing a duel between snipers during the German retreats in the southern sector of the Eastern Front:

> The waters of the Dniester glittered like oil between the front lines. Our own main front and the Russian positions on that side of the high-water embankment seemed asleep, but unseen eyes stared watchfully towards the Russian trenches and bunkers which, lying lower than our own, could be seen into quite easily. Nothing stirred over there, yet over the river death lurked. Now and again the thin report of a sniper's rifle would tear through the sluggish air, spraying splinters off the stonework of our bunker, or the enemy round would crack into one of the tree-trunks in the wood behind our positions. Over there they reacted to our slightest movement. It was best to show one's head as little as possible.
>
> In the concealed machine-gun post of 2nd Platoon, right at the centre of the bend from where the river flowed west, two *Gebirgsjäger* stood with binoculars observing through the camouflaged shooting ports. They had been there for two hours. The ruins of the village

were a glaring white. The observer *Gefreiter* kept up his strenuous searching. Again and again his eyes roved the embankment: nothing.

The enemy sniper must have been near the known position of their heavy machine gun, the shooting port of which was shut. The *Gefreiter* concentrated his gaze. Through the binoculars the embankment seemed close enough to touch. Now – a slight movement! How could he have not seen it earlier! That must be a camouflage net between two boulders and behind it . . . naturally there he was! The shape of the Russian in the darkness of his hide could be recognised as if through a fine mist. Only his face was a lighter, a less dull shade. He was reaching for his binoculars.

'There – there! Three metres left of the machine-gun position, between the boulders!' The observer's companion drew the rifle with telescopic sight into his shoulder and now through the crosshairs he also saw the Russian sniper. Saw how he laid aside his binoculars, reached for his rifle, pushed himself a little forward and – aimed. He must have seen them at the same moment as they saw him. It all happened in a split second: the mutual recognition, the aiming, both staring certain death in the face.

Then two rounds cracked the oppressive silence.

The *Gefreiter* observer saw how the Russian over there folded up – then his companion's rifle knocked the binoculars from his hand. The Ivan had hit precisely in the muzzle of the barrel. Coincidence and a miraculous escape, for all that happened was that the rifle was catapulted aside.

'Whoever shoots faster lives longer,' the *Gefreiter* said after a pause as both lit up a cigarette. His companion regarded his hand thoughtfully. It was trembling slightly. 'You may be right,' came the reply.[1]

1. Braun, Julius: *Enzian und Edelweiss; Die 4. Gebirgsdivision 1940–1945*, Bad Nauheim, 1955, p. 225.

Chapter 7

Towards Defeat

THE APOCALYPTIC END to the Second World War loomed over Germany. Hitler's 'Scorched Earth' order of 19 March 1945 therefore requires no further comment:

> The struggle for the existence of our *Volk* is now forcing us even within Reich territory to employ all means of weakening the fighting strength of our enemy and so preventing his further advance. Any opportunity of inflicting lasting damage on him directly or indirectly must be taken. It is a mistake to believe that partly destroyed or temporarily crippled traffic, communications, industrial and supply installations can be got working again for our own purposes once we win back lost territory. In his retreat the enemy will leave us only with scorched earth and abandon any consideration for the population.

Thankfully Grossadmiral Karl Dönitz – Hitler's nominated Reich-President to succeed him – took on this office in order to control the capitulation, and in an order of 5 May 1945 he prohibited all destruction of property:

> I give instructions that all earlier orders to the contrary are lifted and that:
> 1. All destruction to or crippling of a concern, irrespective of kind, to roads and canals or to railways and communications installations, is prohibited with immediate effect. Preparations already in hand for such destruction and crippling are to be halted. Where such crippling has already been caused, the parts extracted are to be replaced.

> 2. Local measures to maintain public works, the railways and communications installations are to be undertaken immediately.
> 3. Warehouses of food and necessary goods for the civilian population and the corresponding Wehrmacht stocks are no longer to be destroyed upon the approach of the enemy.
> 4. This instruction applies equally in occupied Norway and in Bohemia and Moravia . . .

Matthäus Hetzenauer and his comrades were spared carrying out the 'Scorched Earth' policy as the distance between the Western and Eastern Fronts for the German fighting force continued to diminish. 3rd Mountain Division casualties were so high that such reinforcements as there were could not make good the losses. Combing through the support units behind the lines for men was no use any longer, for they had already been combed through down to the last man. Ammunition was short, equipment threadbare, the mules slaughtered. The troops were spent, totally exhausted, mentally and physically at an end.

Amid the sense of catastrophe felt by everybody, nobody wanted to admit the likely ultimate consequences because the mechanism for survival still worked astonishingly well despite all perplexity and resignation.

Generalleutnant Klatt and his hard-pressed front-line troops received news of Hitler's 'heroic death'. The report brought about no change, for Stalin whipped his Red Army ruthlessly onwards through the German towns and provinces in the east, 'liberating' in the Soviet way the countryside and its population. For many, the Soviet invasion of Eastern Europe meant slavery, prison, years of banishment and death. Words of defiance went through the exhausted divisions, bled to death: 'Dönitz is coming to Prague' – 'Schörner will lead us home!' – 'There is no question of capitulation!'

The war was unmistakably on its last legs.

It was suggested to Klatt that he should remove 3rd Mountain Division from the front and fight his way through to Austria. He

Handshake between Americans and Soviets in the heart of Germany, 26 April 1945.

dismissed this offer out of hand, for in his opinion he thought that it would have a devastating effect on the neighbouring divisions. On 1 May 1945 the division reached Olsa. At this point the ration strength was still 16,000 men. In the operational area, however, all hell had broken loose. At the pit-heads the Czechs had hoisted red flags and joined in the fighting as snipers, for the break-up of the German administration could not be hidden from them. Thus on 5 May came the open Czech uprising by which the Sudeten Germans were driven out of a reunited Czechoslovakia. On 6 May, a day after some cruel excesses against the Germans in Bohemia, the majority of the German corps and divisions pulled back behind the River March – covered by XLIX Mountain Corps

Improvised celebration to mark the first meeting of American and Soviet troops at the Elbe.

of General von Le Suire, and especially 3rd and 4th Mountain Divisions, which protected the retreating German formations against the Red Army.

Now the time had come when Klatt and his commanders were forced to pull out, for on 7 May 1945 there was only one way back into Austria, heading south-west through the gap in the front at Olmütz in central Czechoslovakia. The rearguard in this fighting was made up of tank-hunting vehicles and mobile assault guns while snipers also helped shoulder the burden of the defensive work. In particular the Soviet attacks on Novy Jicin and Stary Jicin demanded the utmost effort from every assault-gun commander. There was heavy fighting at Olmütz, then Soviet aircraft dropped leaflets bearing the text of the Wehrmacht capitulation.

On 8 May 1945 Generalleutnant Klatt was south of Olmütz on the eastern bank of the River March and pulled back late that

American and Soviet officers at Torgau, April 1945.

evening towards Kosteletz on the western bank where he had a lively talk with Generalleutnant Friedrich Breith, commander of 4th Mountain Division. This concluded with both in agreement not to surrender.

Shortly afterwards General von Le Suire, commanding XLIX Mountain Corps, arrived at the command post. 'Gentlemen,' he announced, 'I bring you the order to surrender on 9 May.' Wringing his hands, Klatt advised him against it, but finally the military and political circumstances made it incontestable. General von Le Suire returned to corps HQ through the whirlpool of the retreat and had no further influence on the 3rd and 4th Divisions. He died later in Soviet captivity.

For his part, Klatt decided to press on westwards with 3rd Mountain Division in an attempt to reach the American side of the demarcation line on the River Moldau. Thirty minutes before midnight he addressed those commanders he had been able to assemble to thank them for the exemplary service of their troops. Then he was the last man to abandon the command post and in company with his adjutant, Röttgers, was driven to rejoin his retreating division by the faithful Mathias Schmidt in an amphibious Volkswagen.

> May 9th [wrote Jürgen Thorwald] was a deceptively beautiful spring day. The trees were in leaf along the streets as if they wished to cover the outbreak of hate which at the same time was building up off the streets along which the still battle-worthy German units marched in closed ranks.

Some 200 kilometres [125 miles] separated the rearguard at the River March from the Bohemian woods and the American lines. 200 kilometres was no great distance for soldiers who had come through the strain and stress of war in the east to the very end and knew that they had the Soviets behind them and on their flanks. Individual columns on foot or horseback were overtaken by Soviet units and were lost. But the mass of the army remained closed up on their March of Hope.[1]

On the morning of 9 May at Deutschbrod (now Havlickuv Brod), anti-tank Panzers and assault guns attempted to break through a Soviet defensive barrier. A day later, Generalleutnant Klatt succeeded in penetrating a line of retreat blocked by Soviet tanks, forced open by Major Freiherr von Ruffin with his specially trained *Hochgebirgsjägern* and elements of the *Brandenburg* Division so as to allow the passage of motorised columns. Together with his driver, Klatt made his way to the Moldau, arriving on 16 May but was apprehended by a Soviet machine-gun patrol while Americans on the other side of the river looked on. Matthäus Hetzenauer suffered the same fate as his revered commander.

In the days around 8 May 1945 over ten million German armed forces personnel fell into Allied hands. The victors made no secret of their hostility and ill-will towards the Germans, for their creed was 'Germany will not be occupied for the purpose of liberating

1. Thorwald, Jürgen, *Das Ende an der Elbe*, Munich, Zürich, 1973, p. 301.

Columns of German prisoners marching at the war's end through the endless expanses of Russia towards an uncertain future.

it, but as an occupied enemy nation.' Accordingly the war did not end officially until 8 May 1945, because Stalin, Roosevelt and Churchill had strictly rejected any form of negotiation for an armistice unless it was based on unconditional surrender to them all.

Chapter 8

In Soviet Captivity

THE GREAT SUFFERING of German prisoners of war extended from privations in the American Rheinwiesen camps to extreme brutality in the remote primeval forests of Siberia. If around three million German soldiers fell during the Second World War, another million died in Allied PoW camps. For Matthäus Hetzenauer and all German and Austrian prisoners, 8 May 1945 was anything but that day of liberation which years later the politicians of the German Federal Republic represent it to be as their contribution to 'coming to terms with the past'. Hetzenauer's odyssey led through the Ukraine to the Donets Basin where he became a forced labourer and was reduced to a mere shadow of the person he used to be. He would not have survived those years in Stalin's Gulag if he had not spent his childhood on the steep grassy slopes of the Kitzbühel Alps in demanding work with scarce food. Along with his unshakable religious faith, that was one of the reasons for his survival of Soviet slavery.

Meanwhile, his despairing parents, brother and sister became ever more worried as day after day the postman made his way down the valley with no news from Matthäus. Finally, two years after the war had ended, came the long-hoped-for letter smuggled out from Soviet captivity addressed to his 'Dear Parents'. In January 2005 this letter was the subject of a dissertation which his grandson Simon Hetzenauer prepared for his Westerndorf/

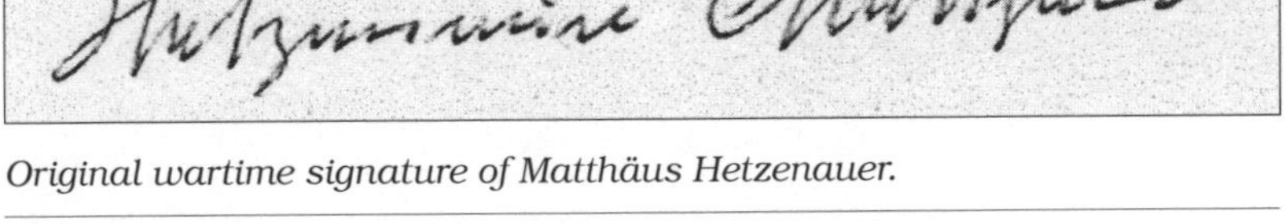

Original wartime signature of Matthäus Hetzenauer.

On the outer surface of the tobacco pouch which Matthäus Hetzenauer sent to his parents from Soviet captivity one can make out the address of his father, Simon Hetzenauer.

Brixental College's set theme 'Young People Research Everyday Happenings and History' for their 'Austria Album'. He wrote:

> The most impressive event amongst the stories my grandfather told me from his experience of the war was a letter he sent from Soviet captivity to his family. My grandfather was a prisoner of the Russians from the end of the Second World War in 1945 until his return home on 10 January 1950. During this terrible time he wrote his parents a letter on 25 January 1947. It was written in the old German script on the inner paper of a tobacco pouch which he had finely smoothed and cleaned so that he could write on it with a pencil like copperplate.
>
> I found my grandfather's manner of expressing himself very noteworthy, for example: 'I have today a favourable opportunity to give a short letter to somebody . . .' This letter made its adventurous way in the shaft of a boot of a released German soldier and then by a roundabout route to the Sonnleithof. In this letter his parents learned that he was still alive, that he was 'more or less OK' but they would not let him come home yet because he was too good a worker.
>
> One should reflect upon the fact that my grandfather spent the nineteenth to the twenty-sixth years of his life fighting in the war and then went into captivity. From receiving the letter until his return home three more years passed, and when he arrived he weighed only forty-six kilos.

Chapter 9

Hetzenauer's Homecoming to the Brixental

AFTER THE HARSH YEARS of gruelling slave labour in Stalin's punishment camps and brainwashing by the Soviet dictator's torturers, where snipers received such 'special treatment' as can be imagined, the traumatised Hetzenauer was finally released on 10 January 1950 to receive the warmest homecoming from his ageing parents and grown-up brother and sister. Then in the parish church and beneath crosses erected on mountain peaks during a lonely trek in the Kitzbühel Alps he gave thanks for his safe return.

At first he led a solitary life to arrange his thoughts and eradicate from his memory as far as possible the horrors he had experienced. For this reason he abstained for years from the pompous Old Comrades' reunions with their complacent clubbiness and wordy platform speakers. When he decided to meet up again with former comrades-in-arms from the circle of former *Gebirgsjäger* it was many years later at the small reunions held by the 144th Mountain Rifle Regiment companies. Thus, for example, in 1999, acceding to the wishes of many, he attended an Old Comrades' reunion at Itter in the Brixental. The group met every year, and 'several of the members in lesser health turn up on these occasions to remind us that we have reached a good time in our lives'.[1]

Five years later the most successful sniper of the German Wehrmacht, who had seen and suffered so much during the ruthless fighting on the Eastern Front and afterwards in the

1. *Die Gebirgstruppe, 1999*, Vol. 5, p. 61.

Brixen im Thale, the native settlement of Matthäus Hetzenauer and his family.

Under the legend 'Dedicated to our Fallen' the memorial chapel at the Brixen im Thale cemetery.

Champion shot Bruno Seissl handing the Chairman of the Edelweiss Comradeship Wörgl and Brixental, Josef Walder, a cup.

An invitation to the Jubilee Comradeship Reunion of 2nd Battalion, 136th/140th Kufstein Mountain Rifle Regiment.

Matthäus Hetzenauer's son Hermann in his hunting room.

†

Der Herr behüte dich, wenn du fortgehst, von nun an bis in Ewigkeit.

In Liebe und Dankbarkeit nehmen wir Abschied von meinem lieben Mann, unserem Tati, Schwiegervater, Opa, Uropa, Schwager, Onkel und Göd, Herrn

Matthäus Hetzenauer

„Sonnleit-Hois"
langjähriger Gemeinderat
Ortsbauernobmann
Ritterkreuzträger
*** 23. 12. 1924 † 3. 10. 2004**

Wir begleiten unseren lieben Tati am Dienstag, dem 5. Oktober 2004, um 14 Uhr zum Gottesdienst in die Pfarrkirche Brixen im Thale und anschließend zur letzten Ruhe. Den Rosenkranz beten wir am Sonntag und Montag um 18.30 Uhr.

Brixen im Thale, Berlin, Koblach, am 3. Oktober 2004.

In Liebe und Dankbarkeit:
Moidi, Gattin
deine Kinder
Hoisl und **Christl** mit **Christiane, Johanna** und **Simon**
Marlene und **Peter**
Hermann mit Kindern **Michaela** und **Christoph**
Christopher und **Felix,** Urenkel
im Namen aller Verwandten

Anstelle von Blumen und Kränzen bitten wir um Spenden für den Sozial- und Gesundheitssprengel Westendorf-Brixen oder für die Orgel der Pfarrkirche.

The obituary notice with which the family took their leave of Matthäus, who died on 3 October 2004 at the age of seventy-nine.

Alles hat seine Zeit –
eine Zeit der Arbeit,
eine Zeit der Liebe,
eine Zeit der Trauer,
eine Zeit der dankbaren Erinnerung –
und für alles was geschieht,
gibt es eine bestimmte Stunde.

In Liebe und Dankbarkeit nehmen wir Abschied von meinem lieben Mann,
unserem Tati, Schwiegervater, Opa, Uropa, Schwager,
Onkel und Göd, Herrn

Matthäus Hetzenauer

Sonnleit – Hois

der am Sonntag, dem 3. Oktober 2004, im 80. Lebensjahr
wohlvorbereitet von uns gegangen ist.

Wir begleiten unseren lieben Tati am Dienstag,
dem 5. Oktober 2004 um 14 Uhr, zum Gottesdienst in die Pfarrkirche
Brixen i. Thale und anschließend zur letzten Ruhe.

Den Rosenkranz beten wir am Sonntag und Montag jeweils um 18.30 Uhr.

Brixen i. Thale, Berlin, Koblach, am 3. Oktober 2004.

In Liebe und Dankbarkeit:

Moidi – Gattin
Deine Kinder:
Hoisl und Christl mit Christiane, Johanna und Simon
Marlene und Peter
Hermann mit Kindern Michaela und Christoph
Christopher und Felix – Urenkel

sowie im Namen aller Verwandten.

Anstelle von Blumen und Kränzen bitten wir um Spenden für den Sozial-und Gesundheitssprengl
Westendorf-Brixen oder für die Orgel der Pfarrkirche.

*trauerhilfe Kitzbüheler Bestattung Sturm 05356/64247 * Kooperationspartner des Wiener Verein * www.trauerhilfe.at*

The second obituary notice for the burial service at Brixen im Thale, 5 October 2004.

Sonnleitbauer Matthäus Hetzenauer zum Gedenken

BRIXEN

Matthäus Hetzenauer, Sonnleit-Hois, Altbauer auf dem Sonnleithof, ist wenige Wochen vor dem Erreichen des 80. Lebensjahres verstorben.

Er bewirtschaftete mit der Familie einen großen Hof in der Fraktion Lauterbach, war stets ein Neuerungen aufgeschlossener Bauer und konnte den Betrieb an die tüchtige Familie des Sohnes Matthäus übergeben, der dem Vater auch in öffentlichen Funktionen nachfolgte.

Matthäus Hetzenauer verwirklichte auf dem Hof zahlreiche Verbesserungen und war innerhalb des Braunviehzuchtvereins Lauterbach ein Pionier, einige Zeit war er auch als Obmann tätig. Er wirkte durch zwei Perioden als durch Urwahlen bestellter Bauernbundobmann, durch Jahre war er Kammervertreter und Umstellungsobmann. Sechs Jahre gehörte der aufgeschlossene Bergbauer auch dem Gemeinderat an. Über 20 Jahre war er Ortsvertreter in der Höfekommission, zudem wirkte er im Vorstand der Raiffeisenkasse. Der Tiroler Bauernbund verlieh ihm 1977 das silberne Ehrenzeichen.

Hetzenauers Leben wurde durch den Krieg stark beeinflusst. Mit 18 Jahren rückte er zu den Gebirgsjägern ein, er war ab Jänner 1943 bei den Rückzugskämpfen als Scharfschütze im Einssatz. Hetzenauer wurde mit dem Ritterkreuz und anderen selten verliehenen Kriegsorden ausgezeichnet. Seit der Heimkehr war Hetzenauer gesundheitlich beeinträchtigt und litt unter den schrecklichen Erlebnissen und Erfahrungen zeitweise sehr stark. Familie und Beruf gaben ihm Lebenskraft und ermöglichten eine ungewöhnlich erfolgreiche Laufbahn als Bauer, als Bauernvertreter und im öffentlichen Leben.

H.W.

This obituary 'In Memory of Matthäus Hetzenauer, Old Farmer on the Sonnleithof who has died a few weeks before reaching his eightieth birthday' recalls his postwar life. 'With his family he worked the large farmstead in the Lauterbach fragment, was always interested in innovations and was able to hand over the concern in good order to the capable family of his son Matthäus when the time came. He was a pioneer within the Lauterbach Brown Cattle Breeding Association, which he served for some time as chairman. He was elected for two periods as Farmers' Federation Chairman, served on the town council for six years, and was for twenty years the local representative to the Farmsteads Commission.'

degrading captivity of the Soviets, died close to his eightieth birthday on 3 October 2004. After a funeral service in the parish church of Brixen im Thale on 5 October his remains were laid to rest in sight of the main porch with the sleeping angel on the death's head of the baptismal font.

The Hetzenauer family tomb at the Brixen im Thale cemetery.

Author's Epilogue

IN THE LATE AUTUMN OF 1983 I was invited by the Hanns-Seidel Foundation to visit the European Parliament where, after witnessing a passionate debate, I spoke with members of the Parliament including the Christian Social Union delegate Otto von Habsburg. On 16 November I spoke with the former Austro-Hungarian Crown Prince again. Our conversation ranged over the mountain troops of the Dual Monarchy with their famed foot soldiers and riflemen, and then we discussed the military activities of Austrians in the ranks of the Wehrmacht in World War II.

Kaiser Karl of Austria, King of Hungary, with Crown Prince Franz Joseph Otto.

Crown Prince Otto with his tutor, Graf Wahliss.

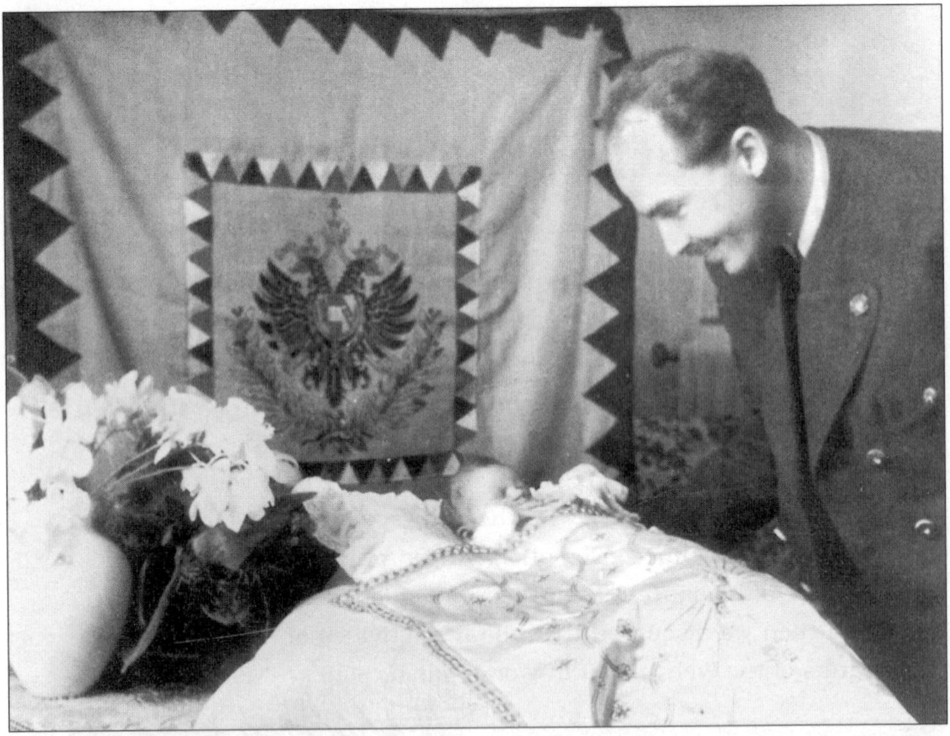

The pretender to the Austrian throne from 1922 until his death in 2011, Otto von Habsburg, with his first-born son Karl.

Amongst other people he mentioned Knight's Cross holder Matthäus Hetzenauer and his own personal visit to the Sonnleithof at Brixental, for Otto von Habsburg had close links with the proud military Tyroleans throughout his life. Later we met for the Erler Passion Plays. Otto von Habsburg was an honorary citizen of that Tyrolean town and over a thousand other Austrian towns and communities.

He broached the idea of writing a book about the most successful Wehrmacht sniper but regrettably I could not help realise this project by reason of my years-long worldwide travels and other interests. Nevertheless Otto von Habsburg always followed my revelations about the mountain troops with great interest.

Some decades later I found encouragement in the successful series *Zeitgeschichtliche Biographien* ('Historical Biographies') and, as it is not far from the Tyrolean garrison town of Kufstein to

HINDENBURGSTRASSE 15
8134 PÖCKING b. STARNBERG
(OBERBAYERN)

22. November 1987.

TELEFON (0 81 57) 70 15

Sehr geehrter, lieber Herr Kaltenegger,

Haben Sie vielen herzlichen Dank für Ihren freundlichen Brief vom 20. November, der mich ganz besonders gefreut hat. Ebenso möchte ich Ihnen wärmstens für das Buch "Kampf der Gebirgsjäger um die Westalpen und den Semmering" danken. Ich schätze dieses, sowie Ihren Brief als Zeichen unserer alten Verbundenheit in gemeinsamen Idealen. Mehr denn je bin ich der Überzeugung, dass wir, wenn wir nicht lockerlassen, unser Ziel erreichen werden.

Mit herzlichsten Grüssen,

Habsburg

OTTO VON HABSBURG

A letter from former CSU Member of the European Parliament Otto von Habsburg thanking the author most warmly for the gift of a book about the Alpine Gebirgsjäger *and his letter of 20 November 1987. Several decades ago he encouraged the author to write a book about Matthäus Hetzenauer*

neighbouring Brixental, I went to the Sonnleithof in the Kitzbühel Alps where the family of Matthäus Hetzenauer gave me an extremely warm welcome and kindly provided me with previously unpublished documents in words and pictures from the family's possession.

Roland Kaltenegger
Kufstein/Tyrol
Summer 2015

Coming Soon from Greenhill Books

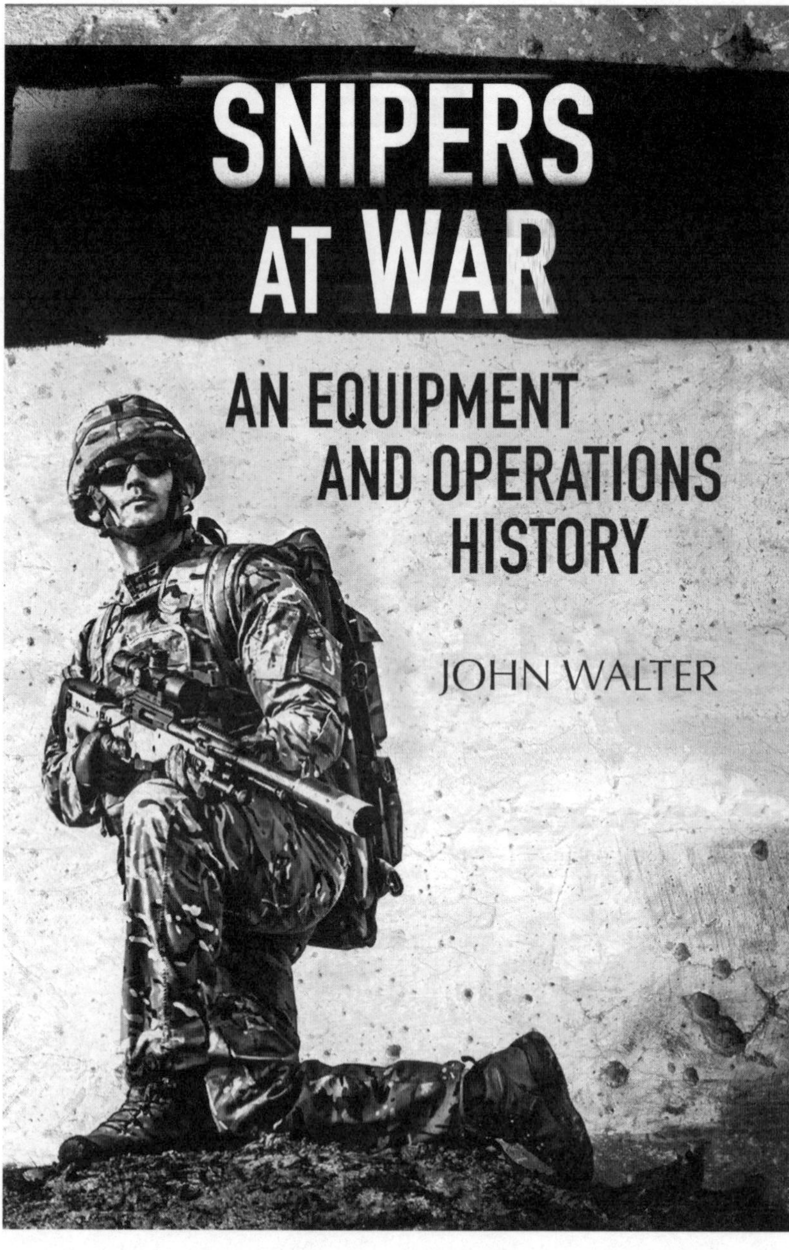
SNIPERS AT WAR
AN EQUIPMENT AND OPERATIONS HISTORY
JOHN WALTER

LADY DEATH
THE MEMOIRS OF STALIN'S SNIPER
LYUDMILA PAVLICHENKO

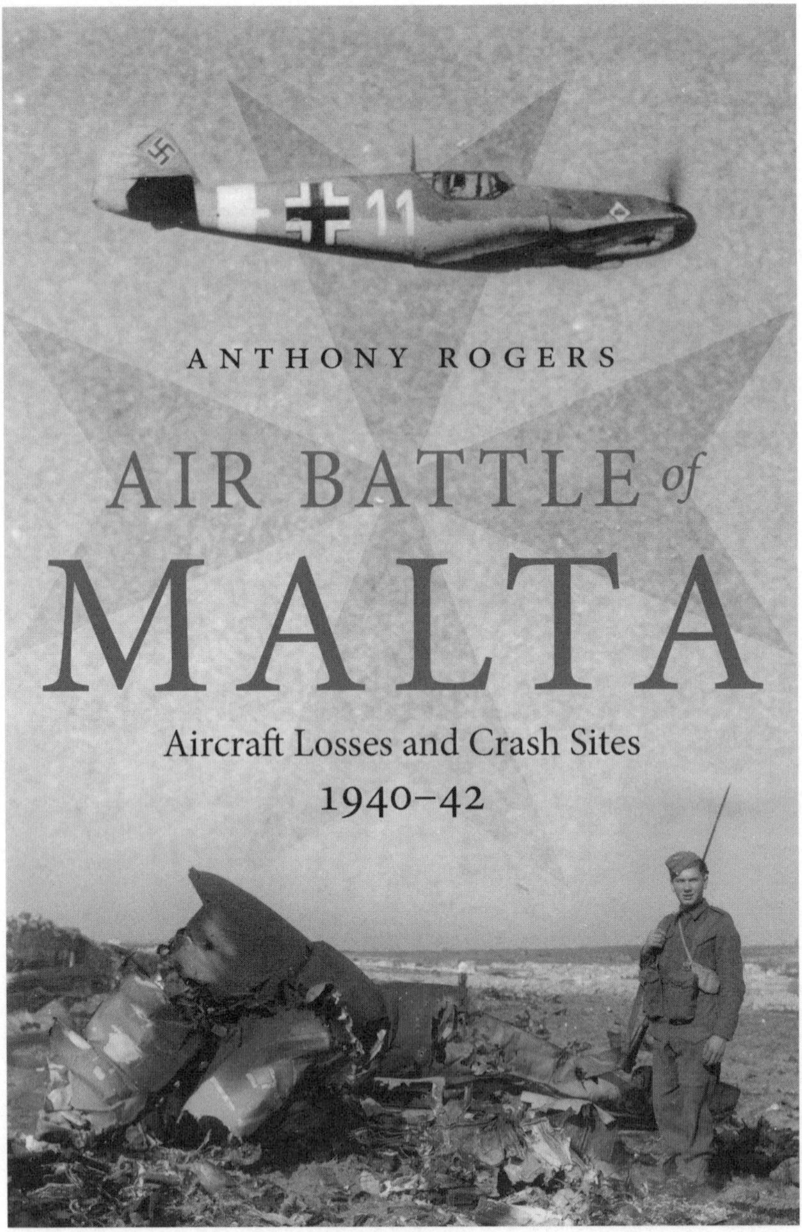
ANTHONY ROGERS
AIR BATTLE of
MALTA
Aircraft Losses and Crash Sites
1940–42

THE THIRD REICH IN 100 OBJECTS

ROGER MOORHOUSE & TIM NEWARK

FOREWORD BY RICHARD OVERY

The
LUFTWAFFE
and the
WAR AT SEA
1939–1945
AS SEEN BY OFFICERS OF THE
KRIEGSMARINE AND LUFTWAFFE
EDITED BY DAVID ISBY